"Can you see anything?"

"Yes, wonderful things."

Lord Carnarvon and Howard Carter
upon opening Tutankhamun's tomb

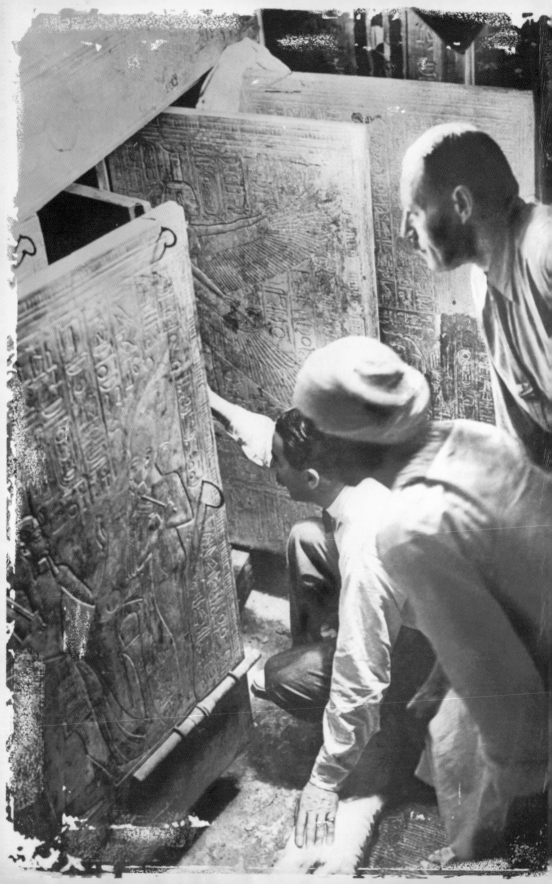

GUIDE TO THE WORLD'S

GREATEST
TREASURES

GUIDE TO THE WORLD'S

GREATEST
TREASURES

MICHAEL BRADLEY
WITH TED STREULI

STERLING

New York / London
www.sterlingpublishing.com

Library of Congress Cataloging-in-Publication Data Available

2 3 4 5 6 7 8 9 10

Published in 2008 by Sterling Publishing Co., Inc.
387 Park Avenue South, New York, NY 10016

Copyright © 2005 Gusto Company AS

Distributed in Canada by Sterling Publishing
c/o Canadian Manda Group, 165 Dufferin Street
Toronto, Ontario, Canada M6K 3h6

For information about custom editions, special sales, premium and corporate
purchases, please contact Sterling Special Sales Department at 800-805-5489 or
specialsales@sterlingpub.com

Manufactured in China

Sterling ISBN: 978-1-4027-6309-0

CONTENTS

INTRODUCTION

There comes a time in every rightly constructed boy's life that he has a raging desire to go somewhere and dig for hidden treasure.

Mark Twain

Somewhere deep inside every one of us the child who dreamed of striking gold lives on. In childhood even one's own back garden feels ever poised on the brink of conceding incalculable treasures. But when we grow up we put away these foolish thoughts and go about the serious and prudent business of being an adult. Most of us barely notice the ground beneath our feet, and wouldn't dream of hiking around a remote part of the world on a hunch. We blithely accept that most of what is lost has already been found and, worst of all, doggedly stick with the prevailing world view about how humankind has reached the twenty-first century.

Fortunately there are still plenty of explorers left. These brave iconoclasts, bounty hunters, scholars, and seekers of truth take enormous risks—exposing themselves to ridicule, danger, and the obstacles created by those who wish to keep them hidden—to pursue their goal. Some seek knowledge, others fame and fortune, but all of them are driven by self-belief, an open mind, and an iron will.

This book will take you on a treasure hunt which crisscrosses the globe, from the salt-encrusted shores of the Dead Sea to a remote cave in the Himalayas via the clear blue waters of the Bahamas and the icy cold depths beneath the Atlantic waves. Travel over land from the sun-bleached sand of Jordan to the nutrient-rich earth of the Amazon jungle.

You will encounter lost treasures of which the combined value is inestimable. But there are also great riches of another kind. The most intriguing discoveries challenge the very foundations of our knowledge of the world and our ancestors. Every year lost treasures are still being discovered which force us to re-examine our place in the world and even in the universe. Treasure hunting is so much more than filling glass cases in museums and pockets with gold.

Many artifacts in this book demonstrate a technical ability and level of knowledge which wasn't available to our ancestors. There are others whose very existence is an enigma, since they appear to have been made before humans walked the earth. Some inhabit a gray area between hoax, superstition, legend, and the metaphysical. But one thing is certain: if you have ever sunk a spade into the ground with the intention of doing more than merely digging a hole, then this is the book for you.

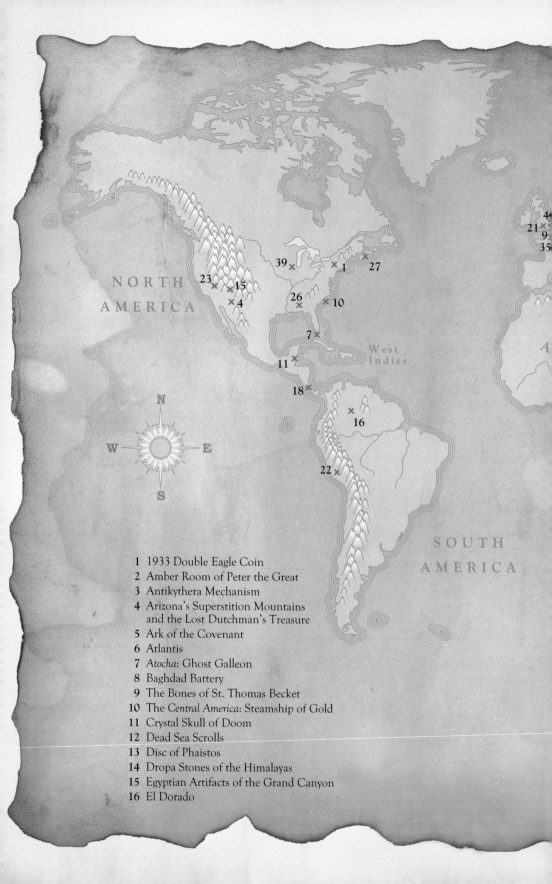

NORTH
AMERICA

39

23   15
    4

1   27

26   10

7

West
Indies

11

18

16

22

SOUTH
AMERICA

4
21
9
35

2

37

42

44 41 31 29

6 34

3 32 5 33

13 36 8

38

20 12

17 30

43 Arabia

25

19

14

24

45 East
Indies

E U R O P E

A S I A

A F R I C A

1933 DOUBLE EAGLE COIN

What is it?

Double Eagles were $20 gold coins minted between the years 1850 and 1933. They show a standing liberty figure on one side and an eagle on the other. They were called Double Eagles because the largest coin until the time of the California Gold Rush was $10. Today they are the rarest and most valuable coins in the world.

How many were made?

In 1933, when Franklin Roosevelt became president of the United States, he immediately took the nation off the gold standard so that the economy could begin to recover from the Great Depression. He recalled all gold coins in circulation, and it became illegal to own them. Most citizens turned in their gold coins to the banks, but meanwhile, the U.S. Mint had made 445,000 new 1933 $20 coins. They never went into circulation, but were melted down and destroyed.

How many survive today?

Originally it was thought that all but two had been destroyed; these had been entrusted to the Smithsonian Institution for historic preservation. However, it wasn't until Double Eagles started appearing at auction houses a few years later that it became clear that several had been stolen before they could be destroyed.

The American Secret Service sprang into action to track down the now illegal coins. They discovered that George McCann, the U.S. Mint's chief cashier, had stolen ten of them. Nine were eventually recovered and the tenth ended up in the coin collection of King Farouk of Egypt, one of the biggest coin collectors in the world. This coin, and the two in the Smithsonian Institution, are the only three in existence today.

How did King Farouk get one?

In 1944 King Farouk applied for an export license for a 1933 Double Eagle, which was granted by the Department of the Treasury, who at this stage were unaware of the ten stolen coins. Only later did they realize their legal and diplomatic blunder. The coin was illegal and was stolen property, but the height of the Second World War was not the most appropriate time to kick up a diplomatic fuss, when Egypt held such an important strategic position in the middle of the Mediterranean. So the CIA waited until Farouk was overthrown in 1952 and his coin collection came up for auction.

However, shortly after the U.S. government officially instructed the Egyptian government to remove the stolen coin from the auction and to return it to the United States, the coin vanished for almost half a century. It resurfaced in 1996, when a respected and leading British coin dealer, Stephen Fenton, brought a 1933 gold Double Eagle to the Waldorf Astoria Hotel in New York to sell to American collectors. The collectors were federal agents, Fenton was arrested, and the coin was seized. It is believed to be the same coin from Farouk's collection.

Up for auction

Fenton was released from jail and he fought in court to clear his name and to prove ownership. Meanwhile the coin was stored in a vault at the World Trade Center. The case was settled out of court, and the coin was moved to Fort Knox, Kentucky, while preparations were made to auction it.

It was auctioned by Sotheby's on July 30, 2002, and was sold to an anonymous bidder for $7,590,020. U.S. Mint director Henrietta Holsman Fore described it as "the most valuable coin in the world." David Redden, vice chairman of Sotheby's, and Lawrence R. Stack, managing director of Stack's, said, "The story of this coin is one of the great numismatic mysteries of all time." It is now on display at the Federal Reserve Bank of New York.

The coin is now legal tender. After the auction, the U.S. Mint officially transferred full, legal ownership of the coin, making it the only 1933 Double Eagle to be authorized for private ownership. Any others in circulation are still illegal stolen property, and the Treasury Department has issued a strong statement saying that if any more of them are discovered, they will be seized and destroyed.

AMBER ROOM OF PETER THE GREAT

What is it?

The Amber Room of Peter the Great is a series of elaborately carved amber panels, including four allegorical Florentine mosaics made of semiprecious stones. The Amber Room, as it became known, was presented as an unwanted gift to Tsar Peter the Great in 1716 by its original owner, Prussia's King Frederick William I, and was installed in the Yekaterinsky Palace in Tsarskoe Selo, just outside St. Petersburg.

It covered an area of 600 square feet and used over 100,000 pieces of carved amber paneling, arranged in three tiers. Art historians Konstantin Akinsha and Grigorii Kozlov describe its beauty: "The room was dazzling. It was illuminated by 565 candles whose light was reflected in the warm gold surface of the amber and sparkled in the mirrors, gilt, and mosaics."

Some have called it the eighth wonder of the modern world, and it was one of Russia's greatest art treasures until the baroque masterpiece was looted by the Nazis in 1941, packed into twenty-seven crates, and shipped back to Germany. Today its whereabouts are still a mystery though its value has been estimated at around $150 million.

Where could it be now?

The Nazi looters took it to Königsberg in East Prussia on the Baltic coast, where it was last seen in 1943. Some people believe it was destroyed by Allied bombing, while others maintain that it was hidden underground by the Nazis.

If it is still lying in a mine or underground bunker, then it is almost certainly deteriorating. Dr. Alexander Shedrinsky, a Russian amber expert and professor of conservation at New York University, fears for its safety: "If the Amber Room lies hidden somewhere, it is most probably in some damp mine, which means it is almost certainly in a state of ruin. Even before it was stolen, it was in poor shape, in need of restoration, and the amber pieces were falling out."

After the war, the German official entrusted with taking care of the crates said that they had been destroyed in a castle during a fire; others believe the treasure is lying somewhere at the bottom of the Baltic Sea, and that it was being transported on a steamer that was torpedoed and sank. Another theory holds that it is hidden in an abandoned mine in Thuringia in the middle of Germany. But there are a host of other possible hiding places—breweries, bunkers, tunnels, castles, mines, caves, and oceans.

In 1997 one of the Florentine mosaics was discovered, and its ownership is still being disputed in court. Also, hundreds of artifacts originally kept in the Amber Room (including furniture, jewelry boxes, and amber chess sets) were hidden by the Russians, and they survived; they recently went on a tour of the United States.

The new Amber Room

In 1979 work began to make an exact replica of the original Amber Room, but twenty years later, the meticulous work was languishing, and funds had dried up. Then a $3.5 million donation by a German natural gas company, Ruhrgas, rescued the project. The new Amber Room was completed in May 2003 at a total cost of over $10 million and consisted of six tons of amber. It was inaugurated by Russian President Vladimir Putin and German chancellor Gerhard Schroeder in St. Petersburg and featured in celebrations for the city's 300-year anniversary.

The specialist task of rebuilding was overseen by Alexander Krylov, a forty-six-year-old Russian master amber craftsman: "The cutting machines are electrically powered, but still, about 60 percent of the work is done by hand." He and his team had to relearn the ancient skills that enabled Russian and German craftsmen to build the panels almost 300 years ago.

Their biggest challenge was to rediscover the amber dyeing process, which gave the Amber Room its breathtaking beauty. It was achieved by top-secret research at the Mendeleev Chemical Institute in St. Petersburg. In 1997 the men were able to compare their craftsmanship with the recovered original panels. According to Krylov, "We saw that ours was just as good."

ANTIKYTHERA MECHANISM

What is it?

The Antikythera Mechanism is the remains of an astronomical calculating device that is over 2,000 years old. Its discovery has forced historians to re-evaluate the technological ability of the ancient Greeks who built it. Not only is it the first analog computer, it is the oldest known surviving geared mechanism. It even uses a differential gear, which was previously thought to have been invented in the sixteenth century A.D.

Where was it found?

It was discovered in 1900 by six sponge divers who were blown off course in the Mediterranean and set anchor at Antikythera, an island near Crete. When they started diving, instead of sponges, they discovered a shipwreck that had been sitting 140-feet-deep on the ocean floor since it sank in 76 B.C.

The Greek government mounted a hazardous recovery operation, and the same divers were employed to salvage the wreck. During the next year they made numerous free dives without oxygen (using scuba equipment there was too difficult) that left one diver dead and two permanently crippled. However, they recovered pottery, statues, and many other artifacts, including the Antikythera Mechanism, the significance of which was initially ignored because it just looked like several lumps of decomposed wood. It wasn't until the wood dried out and began to disintegrate that archaeologist Spyridon Stais noticed a metal gear wheel embedded in one of the lumps on May 17, 1902.

What was it used for?

The device was originally constructed using 32 interlocking bronze gears fitted inside a wooden case. Much of the mechanism was missing, and what remained was seriously degraded, but it was enough to allow scientists to determine that it would have had a turning handle and rotating gears to calculate the motion of the moon, sun, and planets over a cycle of years, against a background of other stars. A fragment of text on one of the pieces is a "parapegma," which associates the position of constellations with the weather.

However, it was only after the mechanism had been X-rayed in 1971 that the number of teeth on each gear could be counted and predicted, and detailed drawings and models were made to determine how it would have operated. In 1974 Yale historian Derek de Solla Price published a comprehensive study of the device. Finally knowing the precise number of teeth and the way the gears interacted allowed him to work out, mathematically, which disc corresponded to which celestial body.

More recently, a British orrery maker (a designer of clockwork models of the solar system), John Gleave, made a working replica that demonstrated even better how the device functioned. The front dial marks out the movement of the sun and moon through the zodiac using the Egyptian calendar. Two rear dials show the cycle of a single synodic month (the time between successive new or full moons) and the lunar year of twelve synodic months. Still more discs work to a cycle of four solar years and 235 synodic months, which is equivalent to a period of nineteen solar years. This number is important because it is a repeating cycle—the ancient astronomers must have noticed the repeating pattern of equinoxes and solstices and phases of the moon in a nineteen-year cycle.

The gears were designed to get as close as possible to an astronomical ratio of 13.368267, which is the ratio required to express this relationship. They actually achieved a ratio of 254/19, which equals 13.36842105—an accuracy of 1/86000. This is astounding enough, but they also appear to have known that this was the closest they could get without building a bigger machine with significantly more gears. In other words, they were even aware of their own margin of error.

Who built it?

When Derek de Solla Price published his findings in the 1970s, he concluded that it had been built by Greek astronomer Geminus of Rhodes around 87 B.C., a decade before the ship sank. He based this on the fact that some of the inscriptions on the mechanism are nearly identical to writing from one of Geminus's books. However, this goes against the mainstream view that Rhodes, at this time, was in decline and no longer the center of scientific excellence it had once been. Predictably, some people continue to insist that it could only have been the work of extraterrestrials.

ARIZONA'S SUPERSTITION MOUNTAINS AND THE LOST DUTCHMAN'S TREASURE

What is it?

The Superstition Mountain range in Central Arizona extends for 160,000 acres and has a complex history inextricably mixed with legend and intrigue. Even today, treasure hunters have devoted years of their lives and sizeable chunks of their savings to locating the much-fabled lost gold mine of a nineteenth-century prospector known as the Dutchman.

Did the Dutchman really exist?

The amount of legend that surrounds this saga makes establishing the real identity of the Dutchman the first step in unraveling the truth. Jacob Waltz was a German national, born in Wüttenberg between 1808 and 1810, who arrived in New York City in 1839. He traveled to the goldfields of North Carolina, where his dream of getting rich quick was shattered. Undeterred, he moved on in search of a fresh vein of gold to work, through Georgia, Mississippi, and California, where he settled for eleven years. In 1863 Waltz joined a group of prospectors heading for the Arizona mountain range, where he remained actively prospecting for gold until his death in 1891. His European accent led to his nickname, the Dutchman.

During his time in Arizona, Waltz made regular trips to a secret mine he claimed to have discovered in the mountains, from which he would return with a rich stash of gold ore. These trips have been well documented, leaving little doubt of his existence, or of his gold mine.

Where is the lost Dutchman's treasure?

Upon his death, his close associates immediately traveled to the Superstition Mountains to try to locate Waltz's mine, armed with a list of clues he had given them on his deathbed. They returned disappointed, but one of the party, Julia Thomas, began selling false treasure maps in order to recoup some of the money she had lost during her search for the Dutchman's mine. This misinformation resulted in decades of treasure hunting, exaggerated and embellished stories, and legend.

Treasure hunters continue their search of this vast wilderness to this day, although in December 1983 the U.S. Department of Agriculture banned all mining activity in the Superstition Wilderness Area. Moreover, many modern geologists argue that there is little chance of rich mineral deposits in this largely volcanic rock. Nevertheless, modern treasure hunters and archaeologists all have their theories about the lost Dutchman's treasure, spurred on by a recent geological test carried out in the area that suggested the area does indeed hide deep mineral deposits.

One of the first writers to explore this story was Barry Storm, who wrote in his book *Thunder God's Gold*, in 1945, that he believed Waltz had been working a rich mine that had been abandoned by the Peralta family from Mexico, after they were massacred by Apache tribesmen in 1847. The theory that the Peralta and the Dutchman's mine were one and the same is still put forward today. Storm's theories cannot be supported by evidence, but they were supported in another book, *Rain God's Gold*, written by mining engineer Alfred Strong Lewis. He argues a logical case for the Peralta mine as the source of the Dutchman's gold, which he estimates was four miles northeast of Apache Junction in the Superstition Mountains.

Another theory argues that the Dutchman's mine has already been found. In 1894, the Bulldog Mine was discovered a few miles west of the

Superstition Mountain range, and some claim its location matches the descriptions given to Julia Thomas by Waltz. One of the leading authorities on the lost Dutchman's mine today is Ron Feldman, who believes that there probably is gold in the Superstition Mountains themselves and that the Dutchman's treasure remains lost.

Systematic prospecting over such a vast area is impossible, particularly given the current stringent rules governing any such activity in the region. All that is known for sure are the words of the Dutchman himself: "There is plenty of gold there for everyone and it doesn't require much digging. The ledge is eighteen inches wide with pure gold high on a ledge above a gulch and it is well concealed by a bush."

He promised to take his friends there the following fall, since summer temperatures were prohibitive. Jacob Waltz died October 25, 1891. His friends might not have found his ledge full of gold, but as they were searching through his belongings after his death, they opened a box to discover it was full of quartz, sparkling with pure gold.

A Scale of two Cubits and an half.

ARK OF
THE COVENANT

What is it?

The most sacred object mentioned in the Bible, the Ark of the Covenant, is a chest, measuring forty-five inches in length, twenty-seven inches in width, and twenty-seven inches in height. It is made of setim wood (an incorruptible acacia), overlaid inside and out with pure gold, and has a gold rim. Each corner has two gold rings through which two setim wood bars are slid for carrying. On top is a "mercy seat" with two gold cherubim facing each other with linking wings.

What's inside?

The two stone tablets of the Law: These are the two tablets brought down from Mount Sinai by Moses, on which the Ten Commandments were inscribed by the finger of God (Exodus 31:18; 32:16; 34:1).

Aaron's rod: Moses and Aaron faced a challenge to their leadership (the revolt of Korah, in Numbers 16:19–25), so a rod from the head of each of the twelve tribes of Israel was placed before the Ark, whereupon Aaron's rod budded with shoots and blossoms. Thus it was "kept as a sign against the rebels" (Numbers 17:10).

Golden pot of hidden manna: In Exodus 16:33–34, Moses instructs Aaron to place the jar of manna (honey-like juice exuded from various trees and the food miraculously provided for the Israelites while they were in the wilderness) "before the Lord, to be kept throughout the ages."

There is some speculation whether the rod and manna were kept inside the Ark or in front of it, but it is likely that they were kept safe inside the Ark whenever it was being transported.

Significance and special powers

The Ark was God's throne in the Tabernacle and was associated with the forthcoming Day of Judgment and God's wrath. It was covered by a glowing cloud, which God said would be a guiding sign for the Hebrews during their years in the wilderness: "will I give orders, and will speak to thee over the propitiatory, and from the midst of these two cherubim . . . all things which I will command the children of Israel by thee" (Exodus 25:22).

The Ark was a talisman so powerful that the Hebrews carried it with them into battle. It helped to part the Red Sea, and it was carried around the walls of Jericho for seven days before they finally crumbled. But it was unpredictable. Moses' nephews, the sons of Aaron, were struck dead by the Ark for bringing the wrong offering.

Around 1050 B.C., the Philistines defeated the Hebrews in battle, captured the Ark, and placed it in their temple of Dagon, but they returned it after the statue of Dagon was mysteriously disfigured and they developed leprosy-like sores.

Once a year, on the Day of Atonement (Yom Kippur), the high priest entered the Holy of Holies and offered up goat's blood, on behalf of his own and the people of Israel's sins, to appease the wrath of God.

Where was it?

It resided in the Holy of Holies, the innermost room of the Tabernacle, and was carried around the wilderness by the children of Israel before, finally, King David brought it from Baal-Juda or Cariathiarim to Jerusalem, where his successor, Solomon, built the First Temple.

Archaeological architect Leen Ritmeyer believes that Solomon's Temple was built in the Muslim Dome of the Rock Shrine in Jerusalem, and that a rectangular cutout with the identical dimensions of the Ark, found in the bedrock underneath, indicates that this was once the Ark's resting place.

The last mention of the Ark in the Hebrew Bible is in the Book of Kings, written about 600 years before the birth of Christ. In 586 B.C. the Babylonian emperor Nebuchadnezzar II sacked and destroyed the First Temple as a prelude to enslaving the Hebrews. But in the detailed biblical list of all the war booty that the Babylonians took back with them to their homeland, the Ark is not mentioned, which suggests to some that, by then, it had already disappeared.

Where is it now?

Even today, men still search for it—pondering clues in ancient texts and clambering through dark caves. Following are some possibilities for the location of the Ark:

- It could be on Mount Nebo, on the east bank of the Jordan River.

- It might be somewhere near the Dead Sea, on the Jordan River's west bank, buried in one of the region's caves, just as the Dead Sea Scrolls were.

- Possibly it is within a church in Axym, Ethiopia.

- It may still be underneath the Dome of the Rock Shrine in Jerusalem, hidden in a complex of chambers, which were partially excavated in secret by leading rabbis in 1981. This work was discontinued by the Israeli government due to religious and political pressure from the Muslim world.

ATLANTIS

What is it?

The Greek philosopher Plato described Atlantis as an island continent in the Atlantic Ocean about the size of Europe. According to Plato's writings from about 370 B.C., the prosperous and powerful island had been destroyed by a cataclysmic event 10,000 years earlier and sank into the sea.

Plato described Atlantis as a powerful city-state that possessed great wealth and ruled parts of Europe and Africa. It was a center of commerce, with the bulk of its population living in a central city eleven miles in diameter. The topography featured both mountains and plains, with canals cut to channel water to the fields and provide easy transportation to the sea. The climate allowed for two harvests each year, one resulting from winter rains, the other from summer irrigation. The island had an abundance of fruits and herbs, as well as animals, including elephants, which Plato mentioned specifically.

Presumably, the people—and treasures—of the island nation disappeared beneath the sea when the island disappeared.

How did Plato know?

Plato read about Atlantis from the writings of the Greek ruler Solon, which were then 200 years old. In his work, Solon said he learned of Atlantis from an Egyptian priest while visiting the African nation.

What destroyed it?

Plato described Atlantis in a pair of writings, *Timaeus* and *Critias*. He wrote that Atlantis met its demise after a failed attempt to conquer Greece, where the military rebuffed the Atlanteans. He wrote that violent earthquakes and floods over the course of a single day and night caused Atlantis to vanish beneath the sea. In the more mythological *Critias*, Plato blames the disaster on Zeus, who was angered over the Atlanteans' complacency and greed after living for centuries in harmony. Plato also wrote about a temple on the island built to honor Poseidon, the Greek god of the sea, and suggested the first ruler of Atlantis was Atlas, who in Greek mythology was charged with holding the heavens up from the earth. Later scholars surmised that the cataclysmic event might have been a massive volcanic eruption.

Where is it?

Plato's account of Atlantis was resurrected in the public consciousness in 1882 when a former U.S. congressman from Minnesota, Ignatius Donnelly, wrote the book *Atlantis: The Antediluvian World*. The book spurred a fascination with the vanished island that led to numerous books and films, and some of the greatest treasure hunts of all time.

Bahamas: The Association for Research and Enlightenment (A.R.E.) has based its search for Atlantis on the writings of Edgar Cayce (1877-1945), a psychic who identified hundreds of people—including himself—as reincarnated Atlanteans. Cayce believed Atlantis was near the island of Bimini, in the Bahamas, where A.R.E. members have found sunken stone formations called the Bimini Road that suggest an ancient harbor.

Those who argue that the formation is man-made cite evidence of quarry marks on the stones and, above all, their linear formation and the fact that all the stones appear to have straight edges. The counterargument is that it is merely naturally occurring beach rock that grows quickly and fragments into a smooth arrangement of stones that appear to have been fitted together.

Many proponents of the man-made theory accept that the rock is beach rock, but believe that it was used as a building material. French oceanographer Dimitri Rebikoff and others argue that this may well have been the only building material that the ancient peoples had and that the Bimini Road is a harbor similar in layout to many of the U-shaped harbors in the Mediterranean, which are also constructed from beach rock.

In the mid-1970s Eugene A. Shinn, director of a field station for the U.S. Geological Survey on Fisher Island off Miami Beach, proved conclusively that the rocks were natural beach rock formed *in situ* by drilling several directional core samples. He radiocarbon dated the rock to between 2,000 to 4,000 years, much too young for Atlantis. None of this has dampened people's enthusiasm for the Bimini Road. Divers still flock to the site.

Cuba: In 2001 a team of Canadian oceanic exploratory scientists discovered an unusual rock formation in deep waters off the coast of Cuba. This huge landmass, covering nearly eight square miles, at a depth of 2,200 feet, appeared to consist of large stone structures, geometrical in shape and laid out architecturally, that give the appearance of roads, buildings, and pyramids.

The team returned the following year with Cuban geologist Manuel Iturralde. They spent a week on board the research ship, *Ulises*, carrying out further investigations of the area. Iturralde found no geological explanation for what they had now dubbed "Mega," short for "Megalith Formations." They also found evidence on the landmass of an extinct volcano and a riverbed, as well as fault lines, in close proximity to each other and to the ruined city, indicating that it was once above sea level.

Iturralde's findings added weight to Paulina Zelitsky's theory that there had once been an island between the tip of Cuba's peninsula and the Mexican Yucatán Peninsula, which had sunk following a sizeable earthquake, 6,000 to 8,000 years ago.

Cyprus: American architect Robert Sarmast and his team concluded that the lost continent is off the coast of Cyprus in the Mediterranean Sea.

Indonesia: Author Arysio N. Santos concludes that Atlantis was near Indonesia in the South China Sea and was destroyed 11,600 years ago during the Ice Age.

Puerto Rico: Otto Muck, in his book, *The Secret of Atlantis*, suggests that sub-Atlantic geography reveals that an asteroid caused the demise of Atlantis. Muck argues that a six-mile-wide asteroid, which would have had the explosive force of several thousand hydrogen bombs when it collided, could have caused twin depressions 23,000-feet-deep in the sea floor near Puerto Rico, and 3,000 shallow troughs that spread out in an elliptical shape.

Above: *Santorini is destroyed by a volcanic eruption*

Santorini: The most common theory regarding Atlantis's whereabouts suggests that Plato, perhaps through mistranslations, simply got the date wrong. About 1,100 years before Plato's account, the Minoans inhabited the island of Santorini, also known as Thera. The Minoan civilization, based on the island of Crete sixty-nine miles to the south in the Aegean Sea, reigned as early as 2200 B.C. In 1470 B.C., a volcano erupted with massive force, obliterating everything on the island and causing earthquakes and tsunamis that destroyed the rest of Minoan civilization.

Spain: Dr. Rainer Kuehne concluded from reviewing satellite images that the "island" of Atlantis simply referred to a region of the southern Spanish coast destroyed by a flood between 800 B.C. and 500 B.C.

Others have placed Atlantis at various places such as Sardinia, Malta, Cape Spartel, Andalucia, Finland, Ireland, and the Black Sea. British archaeologist Peter James used Plato's mention of King Tantalus as a clue and concluded Atlantis was really Tantalis, a formerly wealthy city in the province of Manisa, Turkey, that was destroyed when an earthquake caused a lake to flood the city. The anagram is a striking coincidence, too.

While there is little certainty regarding the location of Atlantis, one thing seems sure—the quest to find the lost continent will continue.

ATOCHA: GHOST GALLEON

What is it?

In September 1622, a convoy of treasure ships set sail from Havana Harbor in Cuba on course for Spain. Among them was the *Atocha*, laden with Conquistador loot: Mexican gold and silver, Venezuelan pearls, and Colombian emeralds. The *Atocha* sailed headlong into a major hurricane.

It sank approximately forty miles off the coast of Key West, Florida, and 260 people were drowned. The captain of its sister ship, the *Margarita*, recorded seeing the *Atocha* "rise and strike a reef one league to the east, then sink shortly thereafter."

The Spanish based in Havana tried to locate the wreck to salvage its treasure at the time, but without success.

What made discovering the site of the wreck so difficult?

When the hurricane overpowered it, the *Atocha* didn't sink instantly. It hit the reefs known as the Quick Sands, and was carried west by the current. Before finally settling on the ocean bed, the battered hull of the ship trailed gold and silver coins, precious stones, and jewelry across miles of ocean. Occasionally, scattered pieces of its treasure were located by treasure-hunting divers, and small artifacts have been washed ashore by winter storms.

Mel Fisher, treasure hunter

The galleon itself was the elusive prize, much longed for by the avid diver and treasure hunter, Mel Fisher. His search was as methodical as it was all-consuming. Over a thirteen-year period, the quest often reduced him to living hand-to-mouth, and he frequently found himself unable to pay his divers.

Minor discoveries of scattered treasure throughout this period refueled both his enthusiasm and his finances. Along with debris, some gold artifacts, and more than 1,500 silver coins, Fisher discovered the *Atocha* anchor, several thousand feet from the reef, from which point he was able to trace a clear trail of artifacts that convinced him he was getting ever closer to what he referred to as the "mother lode": the wreck itself, along with its hoard of incalculable treasure.

Fisher's sons were also heavily involved in the search. His eldest son, Dirk, captained the *Northwind*, one of two fifty-four-foot ocean-going tugs belonging to Mel's team. In 1975, while the boat was anchored one lunchtime, Dirk took the opportunity to carry out some routine checks of his bow anchors. While diving he discovered the nine bronze cannons of the *Atocha*, lying partially exposed on the silt-bed of the ocean.

This find led to much excitement among the crew and the world's press, and two of the cannons were hoisted from the ocean floor onto the deck of the *Northwind*. As the crew set off back to Key West, their excitement turned to a distinct sense of unease. Several crewmen, including Dirk himself, had previously reported strange encounters with the vision of an old man on board ship. The experiences made the crew uncomfortable. No doubt influenced by this, one crewman, Rick Gage, described how he felt that their removal of the cannons that day would somehow have to be "repaid."

Soon afterwards, crewman Don Kincaid, who lay sleeping in the wheel-house cabin of the *Northwind*, was awakened at five in the morning by the sound of an unidentifiable but insistent voice shouting, "Hey, look out up there!" Stepping out, the voice shouted again, but Kincaid could see no one. Then he realized the *Northwind* was listing badly to one side. He woke the crew, who discovered one of the fuel tanks was leaking fuel, causing the ship to list. Despite their efforts, the ship went down. Dirk Fisher and his wife, Angel, could not be located in time and drowned that day. Rick Gage also drowned.

Precisely ten years later to the day, in 1985, Mel Fisher finally found the wreck of the *Atocha*, in fifty-five feet of water, bearing a cargo worth an estimated half a billion dollars. Fisher became a multimillionaire. But after a search that had taken thirteen years and had cost millions of dollars to fund, as well as claimed the life of his eldest son, Fisher had paid dearly for his dream.

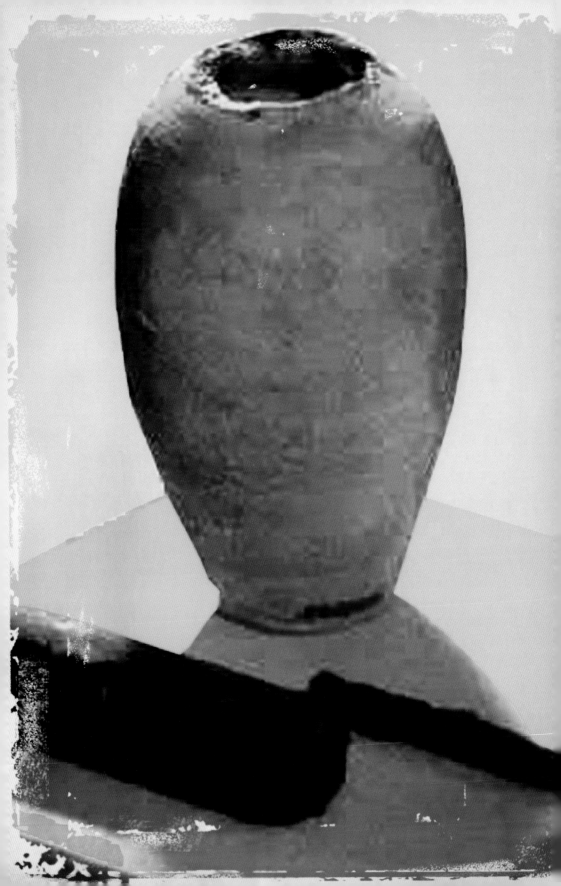

BAGHDAD
BATTERY

What is it?

The Baghdad battery is a mysterious clay pot, five inches long, containing a copper cylinder insulated and sealed with asphalt, through which sticks an iron rod. It is over 2,000 years old, and archaeologists have good reason to suspect it is an example of ancient technology that scientists, until now, thought hadn't been invented until the nineteenth century—an electric battery.

Where and when was it found?

In 1938 a German archaeologist, Wilhelm Konig, dug it up while excavating the ruins of a 2,000-year-old village in Khujut Rabu, just outside Baghdad, Iraq. Others dispute this account and claim that Konig discovered the battery in the basement of the Baghdad Museum when he became its director.

He was quick to publish his theory that it was an ancient battery; then the Second World War began, and his discovery was neglected. However, his was not the only example; about a dozen other "batteries," many incomplete and no two of them the same, have been unearthed in Iraq. Konig dated his find to the Parthian era between 250 B.C. and A.D. 225, because the village where he found them was Parthian. However the style of the pot is Sassanian, which places it later, at between A.D. 225 and A.D. 640, in an era when science began to flourish.

Advanced ceramic dating methods such as thermoluminescence dating (measuring the light energy released from an object when it is heated) would confirm when the pots were fired, but this has not yet been attempted.

How does it work?

A battery works on the principle that an electric current can be produced by placing two metals with different electro-potentials into an acidic solution called an electrolyte. Small charged particles called electrons travel between the two metals and generate an electric current.

Signs of corrosion have been detected on the iron rod, and tests have shown that at one time the vessel contained an acidic liquid, such as vinegar or wine. The copper cylinder is made out of sheet-copper, five inches by one-and-a-half inches, and the edges have been soldered with a lead-tin alloy.

In 1940, a Pittsburgh engineer named William F. M. Gray built a replica of the battery, filled it with a solution of copper sulfate, and generated about half-a-volt of electricity. In the 1970s German Egyptologist Arne Eggebrecht repeated the experiment, this time using grape juice, and he generated 0.87 volts. These experiments proved beyond a doubt that wet-cell electric batteries were being used 1,800 years before their discovery by Alessandro Volta in 1800.

What was it used for?

Several theories have been advanced on its use.

Electroplating: The cells were used for electroplating precious metals such as gold or silver onto a copper base. However, there have been no discoveries of such items from the period to confirm the theory, while there are plenty of other artifacts created using the other two gilding techniques of the time: gild playing (where a precious metal is hammered into thin strips) and mercury gilding (where the metal is mixed with a mercury base and pasted over the item).

In the 1970s, Eggebrecht allegedly connected several replica Baghdad batteries together and succeeded in silver electroplating, but there are no written or photographic records of the experiment, and no other researchers have been able to duplicate his results.

Magic: Dr. Paul Craddock has suggested that several of these batteries may have been connected to create a tiny electric shock to anyone touching one of the electrodes. These could have been hidden inside a sacred object such as a statue or idol to convince worshippers of the power of the religion.

Medicine: Small electric shocks can produce a pleasant tingling sensation, especially when combined with the Chinese practice of acupuncture (small needle-like objects have been found with some of the batteries, although these may have been used to link the batteries to create a more powerful current).

Where is it now?

Until the second Iraq War the battery was kept in the Baghdad Museum. Now its whereabouts are unconfirmed; it may have been looted or hidden by museum staff to protect it.

THE BONES OF
ST. THOMAS BECKET

Who was St. Thomas Becket?

Thomas Becket was chancellor of England in 1155, in the court of King Henry II. He inherited an unruly, unlawful people and threw himself into his role with gusto. He brought the English into line with the law as closely as anyone could in the twelfth century, and, as a statesman, proved his utter devotion to the king. His loyalty did not go unrecognized, and in 1162, upon the king's command, he gave up the chancellorship in order to become Archbishop of Canterbury.

The English Church in the twelfth century was still Roman Catholic, so Becket felt that the focus of his loyalty must now change from the king of England to the Roman Pope. This was to be his undoing. When a dispute broke out between the Church (defended with characteristic enthusiasm by Becket) and the State regarding whether ministers of the Church accused of crime should become subject to civil trials, the ensuing battle sent Becket fleeing for sanctuary with the Pope, then to France, where he remained for two years.

Why was he murdered?

When Henry II had the Archbishop of York officiate at his son's coronation the Pope finally intervened, insisting that without making peace with Thomas Becket, Henry risked excommunication from the Church.

Thus, in 1170, Becket was reinstated as Archbishop of Canterbury.

His first act was to mark the beginning of the end for Becket. He immediately excommunicated all his enemies within the senior ranks of the English clergy: all those who had participated in or supported the coronation. When Henry heard of this he was heard to remark, famously, "By God's eyes! If all are excommunicated who were concerned with the coronation, I am excommunicated also! What cowards do I have about me, that no one will deliver me from this low-born priest!"

Four knights, hearing the king's words, understood this to be a request to murder Becket, to which end they instantly set off for Canterbury. Becket made no attempt at resistance; stepping forward and bowing his head, he told them, "I am ready to die for God, to defend justice, and to protect the freedom of the Church."

The knights split his skull with their swords; Becket became a martyr overnight. Indeed that same night, people began to claim that miracles were taking place.

Where was he buried?

His tomb in the eastern crypt of Canterbury Cathedral quickly became a shrine and the site of pilgrimage. Even Henry himself moved to distance himself from any blame for Becket's murder. He visited the shrine in a hair shirt, lay prostrate upon the tomb, and had the monks of the cathedral whip him as penance. Two years after his death, Becket was canonized by the Catholic Church and became St. Thomas Becket.

The number of pilgrimages made to his tomb continued to rise. His simple tomb was "upgraded," moved to the more prestigious Trinity Chapel within the cathedral, and adorned with a gold and marble altar, covered with precious jewels. The steps leading to the chapel where this altar was housed bear the indentations along the right-hand side, where hundreds of pilgrims climbed up to the tomb on their knees.

When did his bones disappear?

Three centuries after his death, Becket was to encounter trouble at the hands of another royal Henry. King Henry VIII, out of favor with the Church in Rome due to his decision to divorce, broke away from the Catholic Church and created the Church of England. As a result, all things Catholic across the country were wiped away: monasteries, churches, and saints.

In 1538 Henry ordered that the relics of all Catholic saints be burned and that the altars that venerated them be removed, handed over to the court, and smelted down to help bolster the royal purse. The monks at Canterbury Cathedral were given the same order for St. Thomas's bones, and the altar was removed. An entry by the cathedral's archdeacon at the time is said to read, "The bones of St. Thomas burnt this day. God help us."

Elsewhere in England, monks are known to have risked their lives by burning the bones from other tombs, while reinterring holy relics anonymously. The question about whether this was the case with the bones of Thomas Becket has raged ever since.

Where are his bones today?

In 1888, and again in 1949, an unmarked grave was discovered beneath the two pillars in the eastern crypt, where the original tomb of Becket had been sited. The body bore the unmistakable signs of a wound on the side of the skull. However, the 1949 investigation cast doubt as to the likelihood of this being the remains of Thomas Becket, as the wound was not consistent with a sharp-edged implement, and the bones appeared to be from a person of older age than Becket was known to have been. The shallow grave, however, seemed hastily put together: animal bones were also found. There is some speculation today that the grave may hide another coffin or tomb underneath. Certainly, the curious nature of the remains and their placement so close to the site of the original tomb leaves many questions unanswered.

THE CENTRAL AMERICA: STEAMSHIP OF GOLD

What was it?

The *Central America* was one of the most famous steamships in U.S. history. Its sinking was the worst maritime disaster of the nineteenth century, in which 425 people's lives were lost, along with several tons of gold. The loss of the ship hit investor confidence hard and worsened the financial crisis that had been developing throughout the 1850s.

Where and when did it sink?

The 272-foot-long side-wheel steamship was traveling from Panama up the Atlantic Coast to New York in September 1857. Many of its passengers were on the last leg of their journey from California. They were the "lucky" ones, many of whom were returning with so much gold mined from the California gold fields and rivers that they would never have to work another day in their lives.

On September 10 the ship ran headlong into a hurricane from which it couldn't escape. Captain William Lewis Herndon tried to keep the boat afloat, but it finally succumbed to the waves at around eight at night two days later. Nearly all the woman and children were rescued by the brig *Marine*, which came to its aid. There were 153 survivors, but most of the men aboard lost their lives. Superstitious people blamed the disaster on the fact that the name of the ship had been recently changed from the *George Law* to the *Central America*.

When was the wreck salvaged?

In 1981 marine biologist Tommy Thompson and a highly specialized team began to research and plan an expedition to locate and salvage the vessel. Five years later they began a painstaking search of an area off the coast of South Carolina, and in 1987 they struck gold. A rusting side-wheel was the first image that came through from the camera on board the remote underwater robot, and the discovery of the ship's bell followed soon afterwards.

The *Central America* and its treasure had rested at a depth of 8,500 feet on the bottom of the Atlantic for over 130 years.

How much gold did it have on board?

There were twenty-one tons of gold on board. Many of the returning gold prospectors had personal fortunes in the tens of thousands of dollars at a time when $15,000 was considered enough to support a family for life. There were also three tons of gold bars and coins from banks and businesses, but there was a rumor, that persists today, that there was an additional secret military shipment of a further three tons of gold bars.

The most impressive part of the find is a "Eureka" gold bar that weighs a staggering 933 ounces and is stamped with its 1857 value of $17,433.57. It was on display in the California Historical Society Museum in 2001 in San Francisco. The bar was finally sold to a private dealer for $8 million. Many of the other gold ingots, each stamped with their 1857 value, are bigger than anything previously owned either by collectors or the Smithsonian Institution.

There were more than 7,000 coins from the San Francisco Mint, which only began production in 1854, among them the highly sought after mint condition $20 Liberty gold coins, plus lots of gold nuggets and gold dust, which, more than the ingots, brings the reality of the Gold Rush sharply into focus.

Insurance companies claim their share

The gold on board the *Central America* had been heavily insured, and, after it sank, insurance companies who underwrote the losses had to pay out enormous sums of money. So when Tommy Thompson and the Columbus-America Discovery Group succeeded in salvaging the treasure, they immediately found themselves in a protracted court battle to keep hold of their booty. After nearly ten years of costly litigation, the insurance companies lost their claim, and the principle of "finders-keepers" prevailed. Tommy Thompson and his team were allowed to keep ninety percent of the gold bullion and coins taken from the wreckage.

The case was won on the basis that, by failing to keep their financial records of the event, the insurance companies had effectively abandoned their claim. The alleged care with which the salvagers performed their work was another deciding factor. This has angered many marine archaeologists who maintain that it was money, not archaeology, that motivated them, and cite as proof the lack of peer-reviewed published material about the operation.

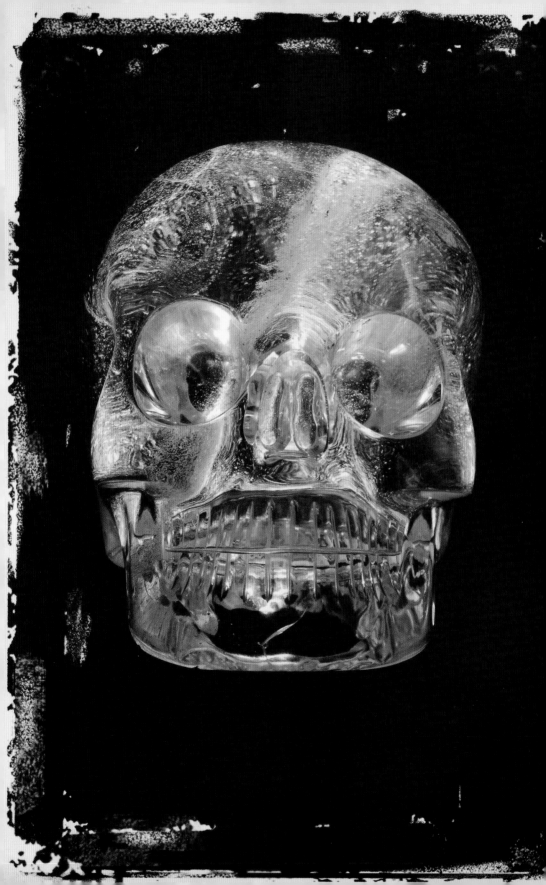

CRYSTAL SKULL
OF DOOM

What is it?

Crystal skulls are replicas of human skulls that have been carved out of quartz, a clear (when pure) crystal of silicon dioxide. There are hundreds of them in circulation, some of them very modern and others carved thousands of years ago. Some have been traced to ancient Mayan and Aztec civilizations. The one which has received the greatest attention is the Mitchell-Hedges skull, also known as the "Skull of Doom."

Who discovered it?

Adventurer-explorer F. A. Mitchell-Hedges claimed that his seventeen-year-old daughter, Anna, found the skull while they were both searching in a ruined temple in the ancient Mayan city of Lubaantun in British Honduras in 1924. The jaw was missing, but she located it in the vicinity several weeks later. It is highly likely that the details of its "discovery" were fabricated and that Mitchell-Hedges purchased the skull at an auction at Sotheby's in London in 1943. However, the skull is, without doubt, very old and has mysterious properties that modern technology cannot replicate.

Special powers

The skull was made from a single piece of clear crystal quartz and is a near perfect sculpture of a female human skull. Here we encounter the first anomaly. It has been carved without taking into account the natural grain of the crystal. That alone ought to have made it impossible to cut, even with modern precision power tools and lasers, without cracking or even shattering the crystal.

In 1970 art conservator Frank Dorland convinced Mitchell-Hedges to allow him to conduct tests on the skull at the Hewlett-Packard Laboratories in Santa Clara, California. Even under the microscope, Dorland could find no evidence that metal tools had been used to carve the skull, despite the fact that the crystal showed a Mohs hardness reading of seven, which makes it likely that it was carved into its rough shape using diamonds, then painstakingly polished using sand and water. But without modern polishing techniques and machinery Dorland estimated that this would have taken three centuries to achieve.

The mystery doesn't end there. The skull has been designed to act as a finely calibrated optical device to channel and magnify light. The bone arches at the front of the skull channel light from the bottom of the skull to the eye sockets, which are concave lenses. Inside the skull is a prism that magnifies and brightens objects placed below it. When Dorland placed the skull over a beam of light the eyes glowed brightly.

Some observers have reported mysterious changes of color. The frontal cranium becomes opaque, and a dark spot forms on the right side and spreads to the rest of the skull, then gradually fades away again.

What was it used for?

Dorland believed the skull was used in a sacred context, maybe as an oracle, and that whichever shamans controlled it would have been able to perform some impressive tricks to inspire awe in their community. But he felt that such an impressive piece of equipment could not just have been made for such tawdry purposes, and he suggested a deeper purpose—that, with deep meditation, the skull could be used to focus and amplify psychic abilities.

The skull is an incredible piece of engineering. The story of its discovery might have been faked, but the mystery of its construction and its optical properties continues to baffle scientists.

Richard Garvin, author of *The Crystal Skull*, aptly sums up this enigma when he writes, "It is virtually impossible today—in the time when men have climbed mountains on the moon—to duplicate this achieve-ment . . . it would not be a question of skill, patience and time. It would simply be impossible."

DEAD SEA SCROLLS

What are they?

The Dead Sea Scrolls are a collection of now priceless scrolls and manuscript fragments that date between approximately 200 B.C. to A.D. 68. Some of the scrolls are almost intact, while others have been pieced together; many are just tiny scraps of parchment. So far, more than 85,000 textual items have been retrieved.

They are a mixture of religious and secular documents written in Greek, Hebrew, and Aramaic, including early copies of religious texts, prayers, hymns, and Jewish pseudepigrapha (writings falsely ascribed to some important or famous figure such as the biblical character Enoch). There are fragments and copies (often multiple copies) of every Old Testament book except Esther, but nothing from the New Testament.

Where were they found?

They were hidden in clay jars in a complex of caves in the cliffs along the northwestern end of the Dead Sea, twenty miles east of Jerusalem. The first seven scrolls were discovered in the spring of 1947 by a Bedouin goat-herder, Mohammed ed-Dhib, while he searched for a stray goat. He sold them to an antiquities dealer called Khalil Iskander Shahin (known as Kando), who sold four to the Syrian Orthodox Archbishop of Jerusalem and the other three to a Hebrew University professor.

In April of the following year a press release announcing the discovery of the Dead Sea Scrolls exploded onto the international academic scene. The race began between archaeologists and Bedouin pillagers to find the rest of the hoard. During the next eight years, eleven of the caves yielded more treasures and many other artifacts, including pottery, textiles, and leather items.

Many of the documents were ripped into smaller pieces because Kando and his Bedouin looters were paid for every fragment that they sold to the archaeologists.

To whom did they belong?

Reading the scrolls has taught scholars much about the religious community that collected and produced them; no one is sure who they were, but the scrolls reveal that the Qumran community disapproved of the Jerusalem priesthood and followed a more ascetic monastic life. It appears to have much in common with other reclusive Jewish sects of the time, such as the Essenes.

Some people believe the collection is the library of the Temple of Jerusalem, hidden in the Qumran caves after the destruction of Jerusalem in A.D. 70. Others argue that this was not a religious community at all, but a Jewish military fortress. It was an important trade route, and it is questionable why the scrolls were overlooked during the time of Roman occupation.

Why are they so important?

They have transformed our understanding of how the Bible developed and have provided a greater insight into the cultural and religious climate of ancient Palestine, which was the birthplace of Rabbinic Judaism and Christianity.

The scrolls predate other Hebrew material by over 1,000 years, and they have given scholars and theologians the chance to read parts of the Bible in its original language, and to compare them to later versions, which have been copied and recopied, changed, and translated.

Controversially, the scrolls also throw up the possibility that the Qumran sect worshipped a crucified Messiah, a practice that was then appropriated by early Christians. The fact that so many of the scrolls were kept from publication for so long has made many question whether they contained material heterodox to Judaism and Christianity.

The Copper Scroll

Discovered in cave number three in 1952, the Copper Scroll contains an inventory of treasures hidden in sixty-four secret locations in the Judean desert around Jerusalem. The Copper Scroll is unlike any of the other scrolls and manuscript fragments. It was printed not on leather or papyrus but on a piece of sheet-copper one foot wide, nearly eight feet long, and about one millimeter thick.

What does it say?

The scroll was very fragile. It was badly oxidized and had already broken into two pieces. It took several months for archaeologists to agree how they should open up the scroll to read its contents. Finally the pieces were sent to Manchester College of Science and Technology (now UMIST), where it was decided to cut the scroll to allow it to be opened up without further fragmentation.

The scroll appeared to be written in an early form of Hebrew. John Allegro, of Oxford University, and J. T. Milik both worked on translating the text and came to very different conclusions about its contents.

Allegro published his work first and revealed that the Copper Scroll contained an inventory of sixty-three treasures hidden in the Judean desert around Jerusalem, totaling twenty-six tons of gold and sixty-five tons of silver (with an estimated current value of around $2 billion).

Is the treasure real or imaginary?

Milik believed that the treasure was imaginary, and he cited a tradition of stories in Jewish folklore that described how the treasure from King Solomon's Temple was hidden. He felt the Copper Scroll fit into this tradition, especially since the sheer amount of treasure seemed too great for any single organization in Israel to have possessed at the time.

Allegro believed that the scroll was fact, not fiction. He drew attention to the expensive medium upon which it had been written, and that the text was a straightforward inventory, without a narrative or literary device. However, his Jerusalem team of scholars refused to allow him to publish his findings, fearing that it would create an influx of opportunists and bounty hunters into the area that might damage archaeological sites. Undaunted, Allegro packed his bags and went hunting for the treasure himself. He found absolutely nothing.

To whom did the treasure belong?

Many researchers believe that there is only one group in Israel that could have had such an enormous fortune and that was Solomon's Temple at Jerusalem, but it seems strange that the treasure map—the Copper Scroll—should have been kept so far away from the city.

Manfred Lehmann believes that the treasure represents taxes and tithes that were collected throughout Israel from about A.D. 70 to A.D. 130 to fund the temple, despite the fact that it had already been destroyed. Temple tax collectors buried the treasure because there was no temple to receive it. Alternatively, it could have been removed from the temple before it was attacked by the Romans in A.D. 70.

Where is it now?

It is on display in the Amman Museum in Jordan. Apart from a small bottle of incense thought to be mentioned on the scroll, all of the treasure is still hidden. Heinrich Schliemann found Troy using Homer's *Iliad* *(see page 184)*, and Howard Carter located Tutankhamun's tomb *(see page 192)* by following an obscure Egyptian papyrus. Maybe one day someone will find the lost treasure detailed in the Copper Scroll of Qumran.

What is the future of the Qumran Caves?

If peace initiatives achieve a settlement between Israel and the Palestinian Arabs, these caves—arguably some of the most important of all the Jewish historical sites—may fall under Palestinian control. Whatever fate awaits the caves, controversy surrounding the scrolls shows no signs of abating since their discovery almost sixty years ago.

Above: *The Qumran Caves*

DISC OF
PHAISTOS

What is it?

The disc of Phaistos is a round disc of baked clay, half-an-inch thick, with a diameter of about six-and-one-half inches, covered on both sides with symbols. It is the most important example of hieroglyphic inscription from Crete dating from the Neopalatial period (1700–1600 B.C.).

Where was it found?

It was discovered on July 3, 1908, by Italian archaeologist Luigi Pernier. It was inside a rectangular clay compartment in a small ground-level storeroom in the buried ruins of a Minoan palace at Phaistos on the southern coast of the Mediterranean island of Crete.

Phaistos used to be one of the most important centers of Minoan civilization, and the wealthiest city in southern Crete. The palace apparently collapsed when the Santorini eruption, one of the biggest volcanic events since the beginning of civilization, occurred in 1628 B.C., affecting large parts of the Mediterranean.

What does it mean?

There are forty-five different glyphs that were impressed on both sides of the disc when the clay was wet. They represent people, animals, fish, plants, and objects such as weapons, and many of them are repeated, making a total of 241 impressions arranged in a spiral. Clusters of signs are separated by lines, so there are thirty-one words or groups of words on one side and thirty on the other. While the script bears similarities with symbols found elsewhere in the ancient world, its meaning and function remain an enigma, though many wildly different theories from both amateurs and professionals have tried to explain it.

It is the only disc of its kind found in Crete, which suggests that it might have been brought from a foreign country. There are details that give clues to its origin, but no one is certain. For example, one of the signs shows a crested helmet similar to that used later by the Philistines, while another looks like a sarcophagus used by the Lycians of Asia Minor.

Some of the symbols are pictographs representing the object depicted, while others are more likely to be ideograms representing an abstract concept. For example, the picture of a boat might mean "journey."

Theories about the disc's text differ:

- Greek linguist Efi Poligiannaki believes the text is a prayer and the language is Greek. She reached this conclusion by comparing the symbols to those from other linear scripts.

- American linguists and twin brothers Rev. Kevin Massey and Dr. Keith Massey suggest that the disc contains a magical text such as a curse and that the language is Indo-European.

- Andis Kaulins insists it explains a mathematical theorem that is "pre-Euclidean . . . regarding the paradox of Parallel Lines, very similar in approach to that used by the great mathematician Lobachevsky, more than 3500 years later."

- Dr. Steven Fischer believes the disc is a call to arms written in a form of Mycenaean Greek.

Other suggestions include a religious hymn, a list of soldiers, farmer's almanac, calendar, legal document, and even extraterrestrial symbols from ancient ancestors.

The most intriguing explanation is that it is some sort of crossword puzzle or board game. It bears a striking similarity to a game invented in the fifteenth century A.D. called "game of the goose." The Phaistos "game" appears to involve taking a journey with the sun god and moon goddess in an astronomical and mythological realm.

Has anything similar been found?

A ceremonial double ax found in the Arkalohori Cave in Crete contains superficially similar hieroglyphics, but the closest contender is a fragment of a smaller clay disc, found in Southern Russia. The complete disc would have been four inches in diameter, with hieroglyphic signs drawn on one side. The signs are arranged concentrically in four circular areas crossed by vertical lines. The ax was examined by Efi Poligiannaki, who dated it to the twelfth century B.C., but it has since disappeared.

Where is it now?

It is kept in a central glass case, in the Herakleion Museum near Knossos in Crete.

DROPA STONES
OF THE HIMALAYAS

What are they?

A collection of 716 grooved stone discs, nine inches in diameter and three-quarters of an inch thick. On each disc is a continuous spiral groove of almost microscopic hieroglyphs, and in the center of each disc a perfect circle, three-quarters of an inch in diameter. They look remarkably like ancient phonographic records and are thought to be 12,000 years old.

Where were they found?

The first one was discovered in 1938 when Professor Chi Pu Tei of Beijing University and a team of his students were surveying a network of caves high in the mountains of Baian-Kara-Ula on the border between China and Tibet.

The caves appeared to have been man-made, with squared-off glazed walls, as if they had been created using extreme heat. Inside the caves they discovered a collection of graves, arranged in neat lines, and they dug up skeletons of tiny bodies less than four feet long with oversized heads. At first they thought they had discovered a new species of mountain gorilla, but as Professor Chi Pu Tei pointed out, "Apes do not bury each other."

On the floor of the cave they also discovered a small stone disc; it was the first of the Dropa Stones. The remaining stones were found in the same caves on a return expedition in 1965.

What do the discs say?

The meaning of the glyphs on the first disc was impenetrable, and it was filed away for twenty years, until Dr. Tsum Um Nui finally broke the code and deciphered them in 1962. After the other discs were discovered they unfolded a disturbing and fantastical story, which was so controversial that the Peking Academy of Pre-History initially prevented him from publishing his results. He eventually published under the eccentric title, "The Grooved Script Concerning Spaceships Which, as Recorded on the Discs, Landed on Earth 12,000 Years Ago." Not surprisingly, the story was not taken seriously in the West and died a quick death.

Whoever created the stone discs referred to themselves as the Dropas. They were a people who had come down from the clouds in a spaceship and had crash-landed in these remote and inaccessible mountains. They could not repair their ship. They described their appearance, which corresponded to the skeletons found in the caves. Their experience was not a happy one—they were hunted down by the neighboring tribes, who considered them ugly and dangerous. Finally they managed to use sign language to communicate their peaceful intentions.

This corresponds with an oral legend in the area of small men with thin yellow faces and bright blue eyes who came down from the clouds a long time ago.

Cave paintings were also discovered showing the sun and the moon and a set of stars, joined together by dots.

Are they an ancient analog recording device?

Russian scientists tested the stones and discovered that they contained high levels of cobalt and other metallic elements. When they were placed on a turntable and subjected to high frequency sound waves, they began to oscillate and showed indications that, at one time, they had been electrically charged or had formed part of an electric circuit.

Are the Dropa alive today?

The area around the caves is still occupied by two tribes who call themselves the Dropa and the Han. Anthropologically they are neither Chinese nor Tibetan. Both tribes measure between three-feet six-inches and four-feet seven-inches and are yellow-skinned, with thin bodies, disproportionately large heads, and bright blue eyes, which is an atypical Asian trait.

One more piece of evidence appeared in 1995 when a report from China claimed that a new tribe of people had been discovered in the Baian-Kara-Ula mountains, with 120 members who were less than three-feet ten-inches tall, and the smallest adult two-feet one-inch.

Debate continues today whether the Dropa Stones were created by extraterrestrials or were merely part of an elaborate creation myth by the indigenous tribes.

EGYPTIAN ARTIFACTS OF THE GRAND CANYON

What are they?

On April 5, 1909, the *Phoenix Gazette* published a lengthy front-page article describing the discoveries of a team of scientists, led by Professor S. A. Jordan and G. E. Kinkaid of the Smithsonian Institution. The article described Jordan's expedition in the Grand Canyon, in search of minerals. What they claimed to have discovered was of far greater significance than minerals.

The article claimed that the men stumbled upon a labyrinth of tunnels leading off a central vault, about a mile below the surface of the Grand Canyon. There were several hundred rooms radiating off the vault, in which they found highly sophisticated copper weaponry, wall art, and hieroglyphs reminiscent of both ancient Hindi and Egyptian civilizations. They said that the network of rooms and tunnels included a crypt, where tiers of male mummies were stacked, each on its own shelf, hewn into the rock face. Each mummy was positioned next to a copper urn or cup and a broken sword. The higher up the mummies were positioned, the more sophisticated the urn, indicating that they were of a later period.

Many of the artifacts were of hardened copper, something that could only have been achieved via a highly sophisticated smelting process. They found "workshops" with evidence of smelting, along with a gray metal that the early twentieth-century scientists could not identify, but described as resembling platinum. A cement-like material had been used to construct rounded grain stores, full of various kinds of seeds. One of the grain stores was perched on a ledge twelve feet up in the rock, and two copper hooks were visible on the wall, as if to attach a ladder of sorts in order to access the grain.

Throughout the tunnels there were carved objects and stone tablets filled with hieroglyphs, all of which the scientists described as being of ancient Egyptian or Hindi origin. Jordan and Kinkaid also discovered a shrine with a large image of a deity closely resembling early images of the Buddha.

The men said they could not find any evidence of bedding, animal remains, or clothing, but found one large room that they felt resembled an eating area, as it appeared to have been filled with cooking utensils.

Why is the find so special?

To have uncovered archaeological evidence on the North American continent that suggested early civilizations crossed the Atlantic or Pacific Oceans long before Columbus represented a major twist in modern interpretations of the past. Traditionally, the indigenous peoples of North and South America were believed to have been descended from Ice Age explorers who crossed into the Americas via the Bering Strait, and that, in North America at least, they lived separately from any other civilization until the time of Columbus.

The evidence of early Egyptian and Asian influences that Jordan and Kinkaid claimed to have found would have shattered that worldview, if substantiated.

Where are these artifacts today?

The 1909 article clearly describes how the Smithsonian Institution, led by Professor S. A. Jordan, would be carrying out extensive research in the caverns and tombs beneath the Grand Canyon, "which will be continued until the last link in the chain is forged."

Recently an organization based in the United States called The World Explorers' Club decided to research further into the claims made by the *Phoenix Gazette* in 1909. They called the Smithsonian Institution in Washington and were informed that there is no record of the discoveries or the men who are purported to have made them.

Today, large sections of the Grand Canyon bear Egyptian or Hindi names, such as Osiris Temple, Cheops Pyramid, and Buddha Cloister. All these areas are said to be hazardous and remain off limits to hikers and tourists and even to the majority of the park personnel.

EL DORADO

What is it?

In Spanish El Dorado means "gilded man" and refers to a South American king and his hoard of gold, which has never been found, despite many attempts by European explorers. It has never been established whether he existed or was a legend concocted by enslaved Incas to send the Conquistadors on fruitless and fatal expeditions into the dense Amazon jungle.

Who was the golden man?

If the story is based in truth, then it may describe a religious rite thought to have been performed by the Chibcha, the indigenous people of a part of the Andes called the Eastern Cordillera. The ceremony took place at Lake Guatavita, thirty miles to the north of Bogatá, in present-day Colombia.

Lake Guatavita sits in a volcanic crater in the Bogatá highlands, an almost perfect circle. It was sacred to the Muisca, who believed that the spirit of a former king's wife, held captive by a fierce monster, lived there. They performed a ritual on the lake to appease the monster and their gods.

Twice a year (others say when a new king was inaugurated), the body of the naked king was covered with resinous gums and gold leaf until he was gilded from head to toe. Then he would sail out into the middle of the lake and make offerings of gold and other treasures by throwing them into the water. Then he too would enter the water and wash away his golden coating.

The gilded king was described by sixteenth-century Spanish historian Gonzalo Fernández de Oviedo: "He went about all covered with powdered gold, as casually as if it were powdered salt. For it seemed to him that to wear any other finery was less beautiful, and that to put on ornaments or arms made of gold worked by hammering, stamping, or by other means, was a vulgar and common thing."

Who searched for El Dorado?

In the 1530s when greedy European explorers heard of this legend, they were convinced that the lake contained untold riches, and rumors grew to include the existence of a hidden city nearby called Manoa, in which even the cooking utensils were said to be pure gold. They put all their efforts into exploring the area, from the central plains east of the Bogatá highlands to the upper tributaries of the Amazon River.

Men like Francisco de Orellana (who discovered the Amazon) and Jimenez de Quesada spent years hacking through dense jungle, killing and enslaving the indigenous people, and navigating coasts and rivers in a fruitless search for the lost gold. Most of these expeditions were expensive disasters, costing the lives of many men.

After torturing Chibcha elders into revealing its whereabouts, Quesada succeeded in locating Lake Guatavita, but he found no riches there. During the next few decades the lake was dredged several times, but only a handful of treasures were recovered. In the 1580s a Bogotan merchant, Antonio de Supulveda, attempted to drain the lake, and today the featureless rim that surrounds it is scarred by a craggy vee carved by his men.

The English explorer Sir Walter Raleigh famously searched for El Dorado in 1595 and 1617. On his second attempt, he sailed up the Orinoco River, but found nothing. His crew mutinied or deserted, and upon his return, his failure and the conduct of his men were used by Queen Elizabeth I as an excuse to have him executed.

In 1965 the Colombian government placed a protection order on Guata-vita to prevent any more destruction to the lake and its surroundings.

Where was Manoa?

Antonio de Berrio, the Spanish governor of Guyana and Trinidad, made three expeditions to the area in the late sixteenth century, and although he never located Manoa, he concluded that it must be close to the source of the Caroni River, behind the mountains of Guyana. This theory seemed all the more plausible when a Spanish survivor of an earlier expedition, Juan Martinez, turned up in Margarita around 1586 claiming he had been living with the Indians for ten years and that they had taken him to the golden city.

ELECTRON TUBES
OF DENDERA

What are they?

They are hieroglyphs in Egypt's Late Ptolemaic Temple of Hathor at Dendera, and they show a combination of elements that look strikingly like electrical diagrams for a light bulb. In chamber number seventeen, the panel at the top shows Egyptian priests using an oblong tube. At least one tube has what appear to be arms inside, similar to modern designs that would allow an arc of electricity to pass between them. The tubes resemble an electron or Crooke's tube, the predecessor of the cathode ray tube now used in most televisions and computer monitors.

In some of the glyphs, the tube rests on a djed, a pillar that greatly resembles a high-voltage insulator. Lines running from the bottom of the tubes look like electrical cords. Each tube contains a picture of a snake, a symbol sometimes considered to represent a glow.

When were they created?

Temples at Dendera are mentioned in Egyptian literature as far back as the period known as the Old Kingdom (2650-2152 B.C.). The temple was enhanced by a succession of rulers, including Tuthmosis III, Amenhotep III, Ramesses II, and Ramesses III. But the hieroglyphs most likely date to the Greco-Roman Period and the rule of Ptolemy VIII Euergetes II (Physcon), the eighth ruler of the Ptolemaic Dynasty. Physcon ruled from

145 B.C. to 116 B.C., and his name can be found in the temple's crypts. Approximately thirty-six miles north of Luxor, the temple is on the west bank of the Nile River. It is dedicated to the goddess Horus, who is seen in Egyptian mythology as the mother of the universe.

How were they discovered?

Although the glyphs are not a new discovery, the opinion that their meaning might reflect ancient electrical technology is recent. Physicist and electromagnetic engineer Alfred D. Bielek identified the line coming from the tube as nearly an exact copy of modern engineering illustrations that represent a bundle of conducting electrical wires. He also identified the djed as a high voltage insulator.

Swedish writer Ivan Troëng wrote in 1964 that "the picture . . . obviously shows electric lamps held by high tension insulators." A fellow Swede, aircraft engineer Henry Kjellson, explored the idea further. Kjellson, who investigated ancient technology extensively from the 1930s to the 1950s, wrote that, in the hieroglyphs, the snakes are translated as "seref," which means to glow. Kjellson concluded there was some form of electrical current involved in the device depicted on the temple's walls.

What are the hieroglyphs trying to tell us?

Many believe the glyphs on the temple wall at Dendera suggest that the ancient Egyptians had developed a method to harness electricity and produce artificial light. A less common interpretation of the drawings puts forth the notion that the tube isn't an electric light at all, but part of an electric motor.

Electricity wasn't harnessed in the modern world until the nineteenth century, and the light bulb wasn't invented until 1879. When Bielek, Kjellson, and Troëng looked at the images at Dendera, electrical diagrams were still a relatively new bit of technological progress. Archaeologists and others who had seen the glyphs previously could not possibly have interpreted them as electrical schematics; they'd never seen such a drawing because they didn't yet exist. Similarly, some glyphs once seen as giant wooden birds are now interpreted as drawings of airplanes.

In 1981 Viennese electrical expert Walter Garn built a functional model based on the hieroglyphs at Dendera. The image of the tube is somewhat pear-shaped, about two-and-three-quarters yards long. It would have a diameter of about twenty inches at its thin end and about one yard at its thickest point. Garn's version worked like a fluorescent lamp, with charged gas.

Ivan Sanderson had an electrical engineer examine the glyphs. Part of the findings that he recounted in his 1978 book, *Investigating the Unexplained*, were that the tubes were positioned at an angle, aimed at the wall. The engineer also concluded that the snakes weren't inside a transparent fixture, but were markings on an opaque tube. That led to speculation that the diagram may not have been for a light bulb, but for a device similar to our television projection systems.

What no one yet knows is what bit of technology is still to be discovered—or how it might affect interpretations of the mysterious temple drawings of the ancient pharaohs.

THE GIANT BALLS OF COSTA RICA

What are they?

In 1940, the United Fruit Company began clearing areas of tropical forest in the Diquis Delta region of Costa Rica. During this work they uncovered a large number of mysterious spherical stone objects. Further investigation revealed that there were forty-four spheres in total at the Diquis Delta, ranging in size from a ball comparable to an orange, to a mass of sixteen tons, around two yards in diameter. Most were made of granite. More balls were found in other parts of the country, including in the hilltops of Camaronal Island and 1,100 yards up in the hills of Cordillera Bruquena. In all, hundreds of stone balls have been found all over Costa Rica.

How were they made?

The nearest source of granite to the Diquis Delta site was over fifty miles away, leading archaeologists to surmise that the balls must have been the work of more than one craftsman. It is thought that the balls may have been made into rough spheres initially by applying hot coals followed by chilled water to the granite, as this is known to cause layers of the stone to peel away. The rough sphere would then have been pecked and hammered into almost perfect rounds, and finally polished smooth, all with the use of granite tools.

How old are the balls, and who made them?

Dating the balls has been a difficult process that has been achieved by examining other archaeological finds buried along with each stone. These bits of pottery and gold artifacts suggest that the balls date back to different periods in history, so that it seems they were created over a period of centuries. The earliest artifacts were of a type of pottery estimated to have been made at some point after A.D. 600. Some gold ornaments dated back to A.D. 1000. Others dated back to the sixteenth century, as they were discovered alongside iron tools from that period.

This means that the balls are likely to be the work of the ancestors of the indigenous peoples of Costa Rica that occupied the area at the time of the Spanish Conquest. They lived in small, scattered settlements of round huts, usually with no more than 2,000 people in any one settlement. They farmed areas of land, growing maize, beans, papaya, avocado, chili peppers, and root crops, among many others.

What were the balls used for?

This is a question nobody can yet answer with any authority, although some of them appear to have been partially buried at the site of a tomb, or mounted on an earth mound near a tomb. However, many appear in clusters, forming straight lines, triangles, and other geometric shapes. There is some speculation that the arrangements of some clusters of balls may have reflected some astronomical configurations; at least one cluster of four balls in a straight line reflected magnetic north.

Much misinformation has been circulated about the significance of the balls. This has been helped by the fact that none of the measurements taken back in the 1940s were carried out with any degree of accuracy. The original location of many has since been lost, making further archaeological investigation impossible. Theories about the supernatural or extraterrestrial features of the stone balls have been largely debunked by the academic community. Claims that the clusters of balls emit radio waves, increase heartbeats, cure sickness, and bestow good luck upon

Above: Belgian archaeologists examine the giant balls

visitors are not taken seriously, but nevertheless result in an influx
of tourists.

Today few of the balls remain on the original site. Rumors amongst
locals that the spheres contained hidden gold resulted in several of them
being blasted to pieces. The government is currently studying proposals
to create a protected site at the area and to attempt to rescue spheres that
adorn private and public gardens across the country and return them to
the Diquis Delta. The preservation of the balls themselves is now seen as
a priority, but their origins and purpose remain a mystery.

GROOVED SPHERES
OF SOUTH AFRICA

What are they?

The grooved spheres of South Africa are over 200 metallic spheres, ranging in size from large marbles to cricket balls, which have been discovered in Precambrian rock that is 2.8 billion years old. According to eyewitness reports, the spheres are of two types, "one of solid bluish metal with white flecks, and another which is a hollow ball filled with a white spongy center." According to one source, some of the spheres have a "fibrous structure" with an inside shell around it that is "so hard it cannot be scratched by steel."

Where were they found?

They have been discovered over the past several decades by South African miners in quarries close to Ottosdal, West Transvaal in South Africa.

According to Roelf Marx, curator of the Klerksdorp Museum where some of the stones are now kept, they were "found in pyrophyllite . . . a quite soft secondary mineral . . . formed by sedimentation . . . " which indicates that the stones once rested at the bottom of the ocean. Others disagree, saying that it consists of clays and volcanic ash.

What is so special about them?

Scientists have been unable to find a natural explanation for these mysterious objects and suspect that they are man-made, especially since some of the stones have a groove running around them; at least one of them has three parallel grooves.

Either these spheres are formed by a natural process of which we are unaware, or they indicate that intelligent life either inhabited or visited our planet hundreds of millions of years before the arrival of humans.

Are they really man-made?

Paul Heinrich thinks not. He has collected data from geologists that suggests that the spheres consist of pyrite, a common mineral composed of iron disulfide with a pale brass-yellow color, and goethite, a yellow-brown iron oxide mineral. He believes they are "metamorphic nodules that formed during the alteration of either clay or volcanic ash to pyrophyllite by metamorphism." In other words, the bizarre spheres were created when the rock was adjusted by the physical and chemical conditions imposed at great depth below the surface of the rocks; a similar process turns fallen trees into coal and diamonds. He dismisses claims that some of the spheres are blue since he says they may have been incorrectly reported by the tabloid paper *Weekly World News*, which he claims has run other dubious headline stories, such as "Satan Escapes from Hell, 13 Alaskan oil rig workers killed when the Devil roars out of control."

Others argue that these "limonite" nodules usually occur in groups that are "stuck together like soap bubbles," whereas these spheres are isolated and spherical, and, furthermore, that they are too hard to be composed of limonite.

Much confusion remains over their composition. Some sources say they are made of a "nickel-steel alloy which does not occur naturally, and is of a composition that rules them out, being of meteoric origin," and the spongy material inside some of them has been reported to "disintegrate into dust on contact with the air."

What about the grooves?

Even if the debate can be settled about the composition of the spheres, it still may not explain the grooves. However, if they are proved beyond doubt to be metamorphic deposits (and therefore not man-made), then the grooves must have been added after they were removed from the rock, since there was no deposit to groove until after it had been formed (unless, as some believe, extraterrestrials were able to inscribe them remotely while they were buried deep in the Precambrian strata).

Special powers

The mystery deepened after alleged reports by Roelf Marx that one of the spheres locked in a glass display cabinet in his museum has been observed to rotate of its own accord, leading some to speculate that they are possessed with a mysterious energy or have a hidden function that we are currently too primitive to comprehend.

HALL OF
RECORDS

What is it?

The Hall of Records, also known as the chamber of records or the pyramid of records, is said to be a hidden chamber holding writings that contain the wisdom of ancient civilizations. The Hall of Records most often discussed is believed to be under the right front paw of the Great Sphinx at Giza in Egypt. The writings contained in the Hall of Records are said to include, among other things, writings from the lost continent, Atlantis. A second Hall of Records is said to exist near a pyramid on Mexico's Yucatán peninsula.

Who found it?

The Hall of Records has never been found, despite highly scientific efforts to pinpoint its whereabouts. The first mention of its existence came from Edgar Cayce (1877-1945), a man known as the sleeping prophet. Cayce was able to put himself into a deep trance during which he would speak about the visions he was having. Those were then written down. Among these writings, which came from a number of visions over more than a decade, are references to the repository, an underground library. The most poignant, as quoted by author Graham Hancock, says: "There is a chamber or passage from the right forepaw of the [Sphinx] to this entrance of the Hall of Records, or chamber."

Cayce made many references to the Hall of Records' location, and those comments—or readings, as they're often called—have been interpreted differently. Some believe there is an entrance near the forepaw, particularly in a spot that is marked by a perfect cross of light on the summer solstice. Others have interpreted the readings to mean that the forepaw points towards an entrance. Still others think the readings mean the secret library is in an underground chamber connecting the Great Sphinx to a pair of still-buried pyramids nearby.

What else did Cayce say about the Hall of Records?

When the sleeping prophet was asked to give a detailed description of what the room contained, he replied that there were 32 tablets. He said the tablets held a record of Atlantis from its very beginning to its ultimate destruction, along with a record of the Atlanteans who traveled to other lands and their activities there. He also said the records held information about the building of a pyramid of initiation and the details of when and how the opening of the records would come. In 1941, Cayce said the "house or tomb of records" would be opened "a few years from now." Many of Cayce's followers interpreted that to mean the Hall of Records would be found by the end of the twentieth century.

What has been done to find it?

After the well-known Cayce popularized the idea that a Hall of Records existed, thousands visited the Sphinx, hoping to find an entrance. Several organizations have made serious scientific attempts to verify the Hall of Records' existence.

In 1973, the first in a series of projects was launched using ground-penetrating radar and other methods to search for underground anomalies in the area Cayce described. The projects were connected with the Ain Shams University in Cairo and the Stanford Research Institute in the United States, but they produced nothing conclusive.

In 1977, the U.S. National Science Foundation funded another project that also involved the Stanford Research Institute. The team used resistivity measurements (a process of driving metal rods into rock and passing electrical current between them), as well as thermal and infrared photography and magnetometry. The team found anomalies at the front and rear of the Sphinx, concluding there could possibly be a tunnel running from the northwest to southeast. Lambert Dolphin, a geophysicist with the team, reported that they drilled four-inch holes and looked under the surface with a video camera, but were unable to find any chambers.

A team from Japan's Waseda University also tried to find the chamber. They were able to identify a hollow about eight to ten feet underground at the rear and a groove at the front that could indicate the presence of a tunnel. At the forepaws, the Japanese researchers found another hollow about five feet below the surface. But no Hall of Records.

Fewer people have attempted to find the alternate Hall of Records, presumably near a Mayan pyramid on the Yucatán peninsula. Excavated ruins are plentiful in Tulum, Chichen Itza, and Uxmal, but the investigators have had no more success than those searching at Giza.

BORT   LANCELOT   GALAAD   PERCEVAL   LE ROY ARTUS

LE ROY CARADOS   LE ROY YDIER

HOLY
GRAIL

What is it?

It is generally considered to be the cup from which Christ drank at the Last Supper and/or the cup in which Joseph of Arimathea caught the blood of Jesus as he was being crucified.

The Legend of the Holy Grail is believed to be Gothic or ancient Celtic in origin, woven together in numerous romances (mostly French) written between 1180 and 1240. They represent a seamless fusion of pre-Christian and Christian elements including a magic castle inhabited by the emasculated Fisher King, a virgin who serves as the Grail bearer, and a male hero on the Grail quest. It is also associated with the Celtic myth of the horn of plenty, the source of all things good—endless health, sustenance, and success in battle.

Early romances featured the simpleton knight Perceval, whose quest for the Grail was successful. Others tell of knights, such as Lancelot, who failed because of their own hubris. The most famous Grail romances are *Le Conte del Graal* by Chretien de Troyes; the German epic poem *Parzival* by Wolfram von Eschenbach; and the Welsh *Mabinogion*. The Grail quest later appeared in Arthurian legend in Robert de Boron's verse romance *Joseph d'Arimathie* and Sir Thomas Malory's *Morte D'Arthur*.

The Grail can mean different things to different people. The term "grail" originates in the Latin *gradale*, which meant a dish brought to the table during various courses (Latin *gradus*) of a meal. Other writers have exploited the old French term *san grial* (Holy Grail) to mean *sang rial* (royal blood). In *Holy Blood, Holy Grail*, authors Michael Baigent, Richard Leigh, and Henry Lincoln claim the Grail is the Merovingian blood line which can be traced back to a union between Mary Magdalene and Jesus Christ.

Above: *Roslin Chapel, alleged hiding-place of the Holy Grail*

Special powers

It possessed the ability to heal the sick, or in Arthur's case, the mortally wounded; it also conferred eternal youth and a never ending supply of sustenance.

Only the pure were able to approach the cup; anyone else would see it disappear as they approached. *Parzival* presents the Grail as a stone which protected the beholder from death for a week and provided sustenance.

Where is it now?

In medieval romance, the Grail was said to have been brought to Glastonbury in Britain by Joseph of Arimathea and his followers. Local legend says that the Grail is buried somewhere under Glastonbury Tor (a hill) in a long-forgotten network of underground tunnels.

In 1962 the famous Grail seeker Trevor Ravenscroft claimed that the Grail lay in the Prentice Pillar at Roslin chapel in Lothian, Scotland. It is now a place of pilgrimage for Grail seekers and many references to the Grail can be found in its stone work and windows. Metal detectors have been used on the pillar and something is buried inside, although Lord Roslin refuses to have the pillar X-rayed.

ICA STONES
OF PERU

What are they?

The Ica stones are a collection of about 15,000 stones of varying sizes, onto the surface of which have been carved a variety of scenes depicting everything from a cesarean section to men hunting dinosaurs. If they are authentic, they would force scientists and archaeologists to rethink this period in ancient human history.

Where were they found?

Most of them were unearthed in the 1960s when the River Ica burst its banks and destroyed a nearby hill exposing a gorge. Thousands of these stones were discovered inside the gorge by an illiterate farmer, who, after threat of prosecution from the Peruvian government for selling these alleged antiquities, "confessed" that he had made them all himself to escape imprisonment. The location of the cave has never been confirmed. The stones are definitely not the work of one man, since it would take a lifetime to carve them all, and even if they were fakes, the subject matter they depicted would require a high degree of education, which the farmer did not possess.

What are they made of?

They are made of fine-grained volcanic rock called andesite and have a dark oxidized layer on them from years of aging. The image is made by scraping away this layer to reveal lighter rock underneath. The rocks are very hard, so carving them using ancient tools would have been very difficult.

What do they look like?

They depict a wide variety of procedures and activities, such as medical transplants, blood transfusions, organ transplants, anesthesia, genetic experimentation, men hunting dinosaurs, prehistoric maps of the world, and advanced technology such as telescopes.

Dr. Javier Cabrera claims that several of the stones show maps of the world with the landmasses in the position they would have been millions of years ago before plate tectonics brought them to their modern-day position, and he argues that they could only have been created by viewing the earth from outer space.

Men and dinosaurs?

Some of the rocks depict men hunting dinosaurs that clearly resemble triceratops, stegosaurus, and brontosaurus, and some even show human figures riding on the backs of flying pterodactyls. This would seem to indicate that early man shared the earth with dinosaurs, a theory which none of the world's archaeological evidence backs up. Men and dinosaurs have never been found together in the same strata of rocks, and it is commonly accepted that dinosaurs died out nearly sixty million years before hominids appeared. However, how else did early man know about the dinosaurs, since they did not have the benefit of modern archaeological finds? Maybe early humans did coexist with dinosaurs that survived, or maybe the dinosaurs are monsters of myth and legend common to every culture.

Could it be a hoax?

The obvious answer is that the natives make them to sell to tourists, a practice which does exist today, but many of the "ancient" stones have an oxidized layer inside the carved grooves that indicates that they were carved a long time ago.

Unfortunately, carbon dating cannot be used to date the stones because that process can only be used on organic material. Normally the age of rocks is determined by looking at the surrounding strata from which they came, but nobody knows where these stones originally came from.

Where are they now?

Most of the stones were in the possession of the late Dr. Javier Cabrera, who kept them in his private museum in the village of Ica in Peru. He dedicated decades of his life trying to discover the mystery of the stones since the time he was given his first one as a gift in 1966. The museum is still maintained by his family.

He was convinced that they are a library of knowledge left by extraterrestrials who, he said, visited the area millions of years ago and taught their knowledge to the early human settlement, which he dubbed "Gliptolithic Man." However, it does seem unlikely that a civilization advanced enough to perform interstellar travel should use such a crude method of recording data, although they are the only objects that would survive so long.

IMPOSSIBLE
FOSSILS

What are they?

"Impossible fossils" or "*ooparts*" (out-of-place-artifacts) are collective terms to describe anything that has been discovered—dug up from the ground, embedded in rocks, or found with other ancient artifacts—which seems out of its time.

There are many of these anachronistic artifacts in existence that question our understanding of the Earth's history, geology, and our dating processes, and even make some people look to outer space for an explanation of their existence. They are of special interest to Creationists, who believe that these items are proof that the fossil record is unreliable and that the world was created just a few thousand years ago, as stated in the Bible.

Some of the items have since been debunked, most notably the "Coso Artifact" *(see below)*; this is a reminder that not all lost treasures have mysterious explanations.

The Coso Artifact

On February 13, 1961, Wallace Lane, Virginia Maxey, and Mike Mikesell spent the day collecting rocks to sell in their gift shop just outside the town of Olancha, California. When they got home and cut into one of the geodes (a sphere-shaped volcanic rock containing a hollow cavity lined with crystals) they discovered a circular section of porcelain, in the center of which was a two-millimeter shaft of copper. The inner layer was hexagonal, and an X-ray revealed a tiny spring or helix at one end. They were convinced they had discovered an ancient communication device, and although they wouldn't let anyone view the specimen other than Creationist Ron Calais, they offered to sell it for $25,000.

Since the initial frenzy of speculation that surrounded the Coso Artifact, as it became known, an explanation has come from a very unusual direction. Chad Windham, president of the Spark Plug Collectors of America, and many of his fellow collectors were in no doubt that it was a Champion spark plug, circa the 1920s. The rock was not a geode, but most likely hardened clay. This is one "*oopart*" that has a rational explanation.

Mysterious vase

Another equally famous case occurred in June 1851, when a metallic vase was dynamited out of a strata of rock in Dorchester, Massachusetts, which was 100,000 years old. The vase was bell-shaped and measured four and one-half inches high and six and one-half inches at the base and was made of a zinc-silver alloy.

Rusty screw

In 1865 a two-inch-long, rusty screw, its threads still visible, was found in a piece of feldspar (very common crystalline mineral that consists of aluminum silicates). The rock was thought to be over 20 million years old.

Semi-ovoid metallic tubes

In 1968 Y. Druet and H. Salfati discovered semi-ovoid metallic tubes of identical shape but varying size in a chalk bed in Saint-Jean de Livet,

France, that is estimated to be at least sixty-five million years old. They concluded that it must be the work of extraterrestrials.

Human prints

A human handprint has been found in 110-million-year-old limestone; a fossilized human finger was discovered in the Canadian Arctic, which dates to the same time; and a footprint that resembles that of a human wearing a sandal was found in 1968 by William J. Meister in the Wheeler Shale near Antelope Spring, Utah when he broke open a block of shale. The footprint was surrounded by trilobite fossils; both these and the rock in which they were found are up to 600 million years old.

Modern human skull

In 1913 Professor Hans Reck of Berlin University chiseled a modern human skull out of a million-year-old rock bed in Olduvai Gorge in Tanzania; yet, modern humans have been alive for less than 200,000 years.

Gold thread

In 1844 *The Times of London* reported that workmen found a piece of gold thread embedded in the rock eight feet below the ground in a quarry near the River Tweed in Scotland.

Chain in coal

In 1891 Mrs. S. W. Culp of Morrisonville, Illinois, found an eight-carat gold chain embedded in a piece of coal. It was later described as "of antique and quaint workmanship." The imprint where the chain had been could still be seen even after the chain had been removed, indicating that it had been there while the coal was forming. Coal formation began 250 million years ago, but even the newest coal is only a million years old.

JAPAN'S UNDERWATER RUINS

What are they?

In 1995 a lone diver, Kihachiro Aratake, strayed away from recommended safe diving zones off the coast of the tiny Okinawan island of Yonaguni. He stumbled across a vast underwater rock formation carved into a pyramidal structure, with large terraces and ramps, surrounded by what appeared to be a stone wall or fence and a stone-laid road. Stretching for miles, the central structure in the site is a "monument," that is itself 1,000 feet long.

Soon after, another diver discovered a huge stone archway, or gateway, constructed from expertly carved and positioned pieces of stone and standing perfectly parallel. The question about whether the site was carved naturally as a result of the action of the currents, or whether it was the ruins of a man-made city, long since sunk to the ocean bed and forgotten, seemed to have been settled.

Who built the city?

Marine archaeologists immediately set to work investigating the site. They discovered undeniable evidence that the central monument had been "terra-formed," a natural rock formation that had then been carved and modified by some ancient, unknown civilization. Steps had been hewn into the rock, and tool marks were found all over the structure.

Then archaeologists discovered the tools themselves, in an underwater cave close to the scene.

The construction of the monument was seen to bear very close resemblance to two ancient castles on the island of Okinawa, Shuri Castle and Nakagusuku Castle. The latter dates back to the first millennium B.C. but is known to have been a site of religious or ceremonial importance long before that. Adding to the mystery, those responsible for building the castles are unknown.

The people of the island of Yonaguni are raised with a myth that has remained central to their culture for generations. Parents tell their children of the Sea God's palace that lies beneath the deep waters that surround the Yonaguni coast. Legend has it that a man named Taro Urashima was once taken to the palace by a grateful turtle he had rescued.

Long dismissed as fictional fantasy, scientists now speculate that the Sea God's palace may be a "myth-memory" of the city that sunk to the sea bed thousands of years ago.

Why is the discovery so special?

Scientists have estimated the age of the underwater ruins as 10,000 years. In common with similar ruins found off the coast of Cuba (*see page 35*), evidence from the end of the last ice age of a sophisticated, civilized society, that was intelligent and could construct elaborate monuments, throws current understanding of the ancient world into chaos. It is evidence that could literally rewrite history.

Until now, established thought stated that humankind organized into civilized societies approximately 5,000 years ago, and, prior to that period, lived in small scattered tribes of hunter-gatherers.

Further underwater ruins have been discovered in other areas of the Japanese coast, suggesting that there may once have been a vast, beautifully constructed, and highly organized city that now lies at the bottom of the Pacific Ocean. Religious monuments, grand arched gateways, staircases, broad plazas, roads, and crossroads have been listed among the finds. At one site, vast "streets" flanked on either side by towering structures, are suggestive of some sort of processional walkways.

The underwater ruins discovered to date stretch from Yonaguni in the southwest to Okinawa's neighboring islands of Kerami and Aguni: a total span of 311 miles.

Ancient super race?

A small but persuasive body of historians have become increasingly convinced that cultural, religious, architectural, and even philological parallels that link many ancient cultures around the Pacific Ocean, from Japan to the South American civilizations in Peru and the Polynesian islands, suggest that, at some point, a mysterious, centrally located ancient civilization existed in the Pacific Ocean, whose civilizing influence then spread outwards.

Many of these cultures have myths describing a great flood that wiped out a former civilization. The underwater evidence off the Japanese coast adds a new chapter to the mystery of what ancient people may once have sunk to the bottom of the Pacific Ocean.

KING SOLOMON'S MINES

Who was King Solomon?

He was a great and wise king who ruled for over forty years from 970 B.C. to 928 B.C., and built a magnificent temple at Jerusalem, which is thought to be the site where the Al Aqsa mosque now stands. He lined the walls of his temple with gold, and legend tells that the source of his great wealth was the mysterious land of Ophir.

Where was Ophir?

This land is described in the Biblical book of Kings: "And they came to Ophir, and fetched from thence gold, four hundred and twenty talents, and brought it to king Solomon . . . and the navy also of Hiram, that brought gold from Ophir, brought in from Ophir great plenty of almug trees, and precious stones . . . so King Solomon exceeded all the kings of the earth for riches and for wisdom" (I Kings 9:28, 10:11, and 10:12).

It goes on to say that although his father, David, had gotten treasure from Ophir, Solomon was the last king to bring back gold from there. After his death, "Jehoshaphat made ships of Tharshish to go to Ophir for gold: but they went not; for the ships were broken at Eziongeber" (I Kings 22:48).

Since then, Ophir has become an inaccessible place of legend, and treasure hunters have, for centuries, sought this lost land.

Prime suspects

Many claims have been made for the location of Ophir:

Peru: The adventurer Gene Savoy, now in his seventies, who has been described as a real life Indiana Jones, has spent most of his life exploring the Peruvian rain forests of the Andes. He has made numerous significant finds, and in 1984 in the Amazonas he discovered a vast ancient metropolis covering an area of 100 square miles with the remains of 24,000 buildings. He named it Gran Vilaya.

A few years later he discovered a set of inscribed tablets in a cliffside cave on the edge of the city. Among them was a tablet bearing an Egyptian symbol called a "Ni-ther" similar to the one that he claims Solomon used to mark the ships that he sent to Ophir. He and his team have since uncovered many other examples of this mark on stone, walls, pottery, and textiles in the surrounding area. He then spent the next seven years finding more evidence to link South America with Solomon, including taking hazardous sea voyages in primitive sailing boats to prove that it was possible to navigate between Ophir (inhabited, he believes, by a fair-skinned, pre-Inca civilization called Chachapoyas) and the East.

Ethiopia: In the Bible, Ophir is not only the name of a place, it is a person, and he was a son of Joktan and a descendant of Noah. His sister Sheba visited Solomon and brought huge amounts of gold with her. Part of her kingdom is widely believed to have included Ethiopia.

According to Ethiopian legend, the Queen of Sheba was born in 1020 B.C. in Ophir and educated in Ethiopia. The country of Sheba (or Saba, meaning "host of heaven" and "peace") covered 483,000 square miles in southwest Arabia in what is known today as Yemen below the southern tip of Saudi Arabia. Across the Red Sea and the Gulf of Aden is Ethiopia, which may also have been part of Sheba's territory.

Above: *Ethiopian ruins*

Sheba had rich mineral resources (such as gold), as well as incense and exotic spices, including frankincense, myrrh, saffron, cumin, aloes, and galbanum, which were in great demand and highly prized all over Arabia. The trade in spices and gems was very active, and the Sabaeans were extensive traders, bandits, and slavers. From here, trade routes branched out all over the ancient world.

The Bible and the Koran describe how Sheba heard about King Solomon's Temple and his exemplary governance, so she paid him a visit. However, this was no weekend trip. She would have spent six months making the 1,400-mile journey through the desert sands of Arabia, along the coast of the Red Sea, up into Moab, and across the Jordan River. She was accompanied by a caravan of 797 camels, mules, and asses, and when she reached Jerusalem she showered Solomon with gifts. According to I Kings 10:10 "there came no more such abundance of spices as these which the Queen of Sheba gave to King Solomon." The spices alone were worth a fortune, but the gold she gave to Solomon is even more remarkable—120 talents, or 146,000 ounces worth about $40 million by today's prices. A talent of gold is 3,000 shekels, and a shekel was a day's wage, so Sheba's gift represented 360,000 days of labor. If she could afford to give that much away in backhanders, she must have had lots more at home.

Author, documentary maker, and adventurer Tahir Shah is convinced that Ophir was in Ethiopia. He has written an intriguing account of his treasure-hunting adventures in Africa, *In Search of King Solomon's Mines*.

Sri Lanka: Journalist K. T. Rajasingham believes that the name Ophir is a corruption of the country of the Oviyar, which was inhabited by the Nagas tribe around Mantai, a city port in the northwestern part of Lanka. The country of Lanka, he claims, was once twelve times larger than it is today. Over the centuries flooding has caused the landmass to shrink, and its name has changed to Taprobane, then Serendib, later to Ceylon, and today, Sri Lanka. He says that Ophir has long since been reclaimed by the sea and any serious attempt to find Solomon's gold should focus on the northwestern coast of Sri Lanka, where the submerged city awaits discovery.

Above: *Ruins of Great Zimbabwe*

Yemen: In 1996 the diamond prospector Chuck Fipke (who, a decade ago, became a billionaire when he struck Canada's first diamond deposit) was searching for gold deposits in the Yemeni desert when he uncovered a network of ancient mine tunnels, which he believed to be the source of Sheba's gold. Larry Frolick describes Fipke's adventures in the book *Ten Thousand Scorpions: The Search for the Queen of Sheba's Gold*. Unfortunately, "What he found there were not answers but more questions—questions that ultimately led him . . . deep into the heart of Sheba's mystery."

Zimbabwe: H. Rider Haggard's colonial-era romp, *King Solomon's Mines*, written in 1885, has fixed Africa in many people's minds as the source of Solomon's wealth. But it was the German explorer Karl Mauch who, fourteen years earlier, discovered the archaeological ruins of Great Zimbabwe, a massive city of stone buildings in the southeastern part of the country. A man of his time, he couldn't accept that blacks could have built this civilization, nor its magnificent temple, which he claimed was a copy of Solomon's Temple in Jerusalem. He believed he had found the home of the Queen of Sheba and her gold. In fact, the city was built by Bantu ancestors of the Shona over a period of 400 years beginning in the eleventh century (in the Shona language Zimbabwe means "stone building"), but it is still Africa that draws public curiosity about King Solomon and his unprecedented wealth.

LOST
CONFEDERATE GOLD

Where was it lost?

Many U.S. states and parts of Canada have their stories of lost Confederate gold. According to Warren Getler and Bob Brewer, authors of *Rebel Gold*, Southern spies across the Confederacy buried millions of dollars in gold across Canada in the 1860s in the hopes of funding a second war in the future. Some believe much of this gold has been relocated around the Southern states. Stories of Confederate gold abound, but one among them stands out and is one of Georgia's most lingering mysteries.

How much was it?

The gold coins and bullion were worth about $100,000 in 1865, when they disappeared. Today, this treasure would be worth over $1 million.

What happened?

On May 24, 1865, two wagon trains were loaded up with a small fortune in gold. One wagon contained what remained of the Confederate treasury, and the other was filled with money from Virginia banks. Accounts differ widely on how many wagons there were, how much they contained, and where they were heading. Lincoln County tourism information says, "Seven wagons loaded with gold left Washington

Above: *Wagon trains were often used to transport items of value*

[Georgia] enroute to Abbeville, South Carolina, where the gold was to be sent by rail to Richmond, Virginia, the capital of the Confederacy." Other accounts say the gold was being hurried away from Virginia when Jefferson Davis fled and went on the run.

Another account says the money was supposed to be taken by Naval Captain William H. Parker and his team to Anderson, South Carolina, and then to Savannah, where it was going to be loaded on a ship bound for France. The French had given huge amounts to help fund the Confederate cause and Jefferson Davis had vowed to return the loan.

Parker supposedly camped on Chennault Plantation outside Washington, Georgia, and rendezvoused with Jefferson Davis, where he was told to make his way to Augusta and Savannah, making sure he stayed away from Union troops who were out in force around Georgia.

He set off and almost immediately had to return to the Chennault Plantation after encountering Union forces. They were unable to ask

Jefferson Davis for further orders because he had already left. Then their party was hijacked by bushwhackers just yards away from the front of the house. They fled with their spoils, but many believe that they could not carry all of it and buried it in locations on and around the plantation. Others say the gold was spread out amongst the locals, and there are even rumors that a large stash was buried where the Apalachee and Oconee Rivers meet. But a legend persists that much of the gold was buried somewhere on the plantation.

Union troops soon overran the plantation looking for the gold, and they brutally tortured the Chennault family and other members of the household to make them confess its location. They were even taken to Washington for further interrogation, but none of them knew, or none of them divulged, the whereabouts of the lost treasure.

After this incident the Chennault plantation was nicknamed the "golden farm," and many bounty hunters trespassed looking for the gold. Many individual gold coins have been washed up along the dirt tracks near the plantation during heavy rains, but the hoard remains hidden.

THE
MONEY PIT

What is it?

The Money Pit is indeed a pit, although in 200 years of excavation, the only money associated with it so far is that which has been poured into the search for buried treasure.

The pit was discovered in 1795 on the 140-acre Oak Island, one of 360 islands in Manhone Bay on the south shore of Nova Scotia, Canada. What was a circular depression at the southeastern end of the island became one of the most dug-up spots on Earth. Early accounts describe the depression as being under a tree branch that supported a tackle block, a pulley used to hoist heavy objects on ships. A series of treasure hunters over two centuries dug at and around the depression, unearthing layers of wood, rock, and coconut husks at regular levels. They found possible booby traps, a bit of gold, and a small piece of parchment with writing on it. But most enticingly, the old records show the discovery of a stone with a cryptic inscription; most Money Pit investigators agree that the inscription's translation is "Forty feet below, two million pounds are buried."

Who discovered it?

A young man named Donald Daniel McInnis found the depression. McInnis recruited two friends to help excavate the site, John Smith and Anthony Vaughn. The three men began digging and discovered a layer of flagstones a few feet below. They are also said to have noticed pick marks on the pit's walls. As they dug, they encountered a layer of logs approximately every ten feet. They abandoned their effort at thirty feet, having uncovered nothing of value and unable to recruit help from skeptical locals.

The mystery of the Money Pit

For more than two centuries, treasure hunters have dug and burrowed through the southeastern end of Oak Island, hoping to discover what riches might be buried in the Money Pit. Over the years, most believed they'd find a pirate's chest, some speculating that it was the preferred hiding spot of Captain Kidd or even Blackbeard. Others have speculated that a treasure was buried by British troops during the American revolution, by sailors from a shipwrecked Spanish galleon, or by the Inca.

One theory suggests that the Money Pit holds the lost treasures of the exiled French Knights Templar, the group later known as the Freemasons. Legend claims that one of those treasures is the chalice used at the Last Supper—the Holy Grail.

At least one contemporary investigator, who spent more than ten years looking into the Money Pit, concluded that the Freemason theory was accurate—in a way. Pointing to numerous possible Masonic symbols in the Money Pit legend and the prevalence of Freemasonry in the area at the time the story surfaced, the theory is that the 200-year-old mystery is merely a Masonic allegory—a symbolic story like those common to the order.

Others, who believe the Money Pit holds something far more valuable than a symbol, have invested millions in a quest to uncover it. And cash hasn't been the only price—at least four men have died in excavation accidents.

Eight years after McInnis initiated the first dig, the three men joined Onslow businessman Simeon Lynds to form the Onslow Company. They excavated further, recording layers of wood at ten-foot intervals as well as layers of charcoal, clay, and coconut husks at forty, fifty, and sixty feet respectively. At ninety feet, they found the stone bearing the cryptic inscription. Soon after, they struck something they believed might be a wooden chest while probing with a crowbar, but retired for the night. When they set out to resume work in the morning, they discovered the shaft flooded with sixty feet of water. Bailing was fruitless, as the water level remained the same and they abandoned the search a second time. The following year the Onslow Company attempted to bypass the water with a parallel shaft, but that flooded as well and they gave up for the final time.

At least three other companies were formed before 1900, but all failed to find anything of significance. Then, in 1966, an American building contractor named Dan Blankenship formed a partnership with Canadian businessman David Tobias. Together they drew in other investors, forming the Triton Alliance, which built a 200-meter causeway to the island and conducted extensive excavation with heavy machinery. Their projected $10 million "big dig" was thwarted by land disputes, mechanical problems, a sinking stock market in 1987, and, eventually, a falling out among the partners.

No longer open to tourists, the Money Pit continues to keep its treasures secret.

NAZI GOLD

What is it?

It has been described as "one of the greatest thefts by a government in history." Nazi Germany confiscated about $580 million of central bank gold, looted from the banks of countries it had invaded and civilians murdered in the concentration camps and stripped of their belongings ranging from gold teeth to rings and other valuables. At the end of the war, the western allies recovered large amounts of gold, but hundreds of millions of dollars worth are still missing.

How did they do it?

From 1939 onwards, the gold the Nazis had stolen was sold to neutral countries such as Switzerland, Sweden, Portugal, and Turkey. Much of the gold had been melted down and issued with fake pre-war hallmarks. Without the help of these "neutral" countries, Hitler could not have financed his war.

Where was it hidden?

In February 1945, the majority of the remaining gold reserves was transported from the Reichsbank in Berlin, after it was bombed, to a potassium mine deep underneath the village of Merkers, 200 miles to the southwest. It was also used to store looted art treasures. The total value was about $520 million. This was recovered by the Allies.

In April 1945, the remaining contents of the Reichsbank—nine tons of gold, hundreds of sacks of foreign currency, and other treasures—were sent to Oberbayern in the mountains of southern Bavaria. This treasure was hidden somewhere around Lake Walchensee. After the war only about three-quarters of this stash was recovered.

Swiss Banks

By far the largest amount of unrecovered gold is still sitting in Swiss banks. According to a report compiled by the Swiss Bergier Commission and U.S. Justice Department's Office of Special Investigations, this has been estimated at about $4 billion, of which $2.8 billion was stolen. The report also estimated that 75 percent of Nazi gold transactions went through Switzerland, although the country has only admitted to buying 1.2 billion Swiss francs worth of gold. The commission also concluded that the Nazis had stolen $146 million in gold from Holocaust victims.

The Swiss also held Nazi accounts and thousands more were opened by German Jews attempting to protect their money. For fifty years after the war, the relatives of those who had opened these accounts and perished in the camps were stonewalled by the Swiss banks, on the grounds that there was no paperwork or death certificates. Finally, in 1997, the Swiss, under pressure from the U.S., announced that they would set up a humanitarian fund of $70 million, but this is still only a fraction of what lies unclaimed and undisclosed in bank vaults in Switzerland. Jewish organizations believe it could run into the billions. Swiss banks have now made a list of dormant accounts accessible to the public, and an international panel has been set up to adjudicate valid claims.

What happened to the recovered gold?

At the end of the war, gold which was clearly from death camp victims was used to help survivors. The gold bars were divided up among the ten looted countries, but individual claims for gold were not permitted, on the basis that it would be too difficult to administer.

NOAH'S ARK

What is it?

According to the biblical Book of Genesis, 4,300 years ago God instructed Noah to build an ark: "Make thee an ark of gopher wood; rooms shalt though make in the ark . . . the length of the ark shall be three hundred cubits [450 feet], the breadth of it fifty cubits [75 feet], and the height of it thirty cubits [45 feet]. A window shalt thou make in the ark, and in a cubit shalt thou finish it above; and the door of the ark shalt thou set in the side therof " (Genesis 6:14).

Noah collected two of every animal, and when the Great Flood came he sailed with his family for forty days and nights, finally coming to rest on Mount Ararat, an extinct volcano in Turkey, close to the border with modern-day Iran and Armenia.

Could it be true?

Modern scientists have found geographical evidence proving that there was a catastrophic flood that affected a large part of the world around this time.

Maritime experts have said that the Ark would have had a large capacity and would have been very stable in water. The total volume would have

been 1,518,000 cubic feet, which is equivalent to the capacity of 569 modern railroad stock cars. John C. Whitcomb and Henry M. Morris, in their book, *The Genesis Flood*, believe that Noah would have needed to accommodate only about 35,000 individual animals to cover most of the land-based species.

Some people claim that collecting the animals might have been made easier by the herding instinct of animals when a natural disaster is imminent, and feeding them might not have been a burden since many animals go into a latent state of hibernation during times of crisis.

So whether or not one believes in the biblical account of Noah, it is very likely that there was a flood in that part of the world and that the Ark was seaworthy. Also, Ararat is the highest mountain in the area, so it would have been the first land to show when the waters receded.

Ark sightings

There have been many searches for and sightings of the Ark, and the first written report is 700 years old.

Marco Polo: In the thirteenth century, this great explorer wrote an account of his sighting in his book, *The Travels of Marco Polo*: "In the heart of Greater Armenia is a very high mountain, shaped like a cube (or cup), on which Noah's ark is said to have rested, whence it is called the Mountain of Noah's Ark . . . On the summit the snow lies so deep all the year round that no one can ever climb it; this snow never entirely melts, but new snow is for ever falling on the old, so that the level rises."

Viscount James Bryce: In 1876, this British diplomat climbed Mt. Ararat and reported in his book, *Transcaucasia and Ararat*: "I saw at a height of over 13,000 feet, lying on the loose blocks, a piece of wood about four feet long and five inches thick, evidently cut by some tool, and so far above the limit of trees that it could not possibly be a natural fragment." He concluded, "This wood, therefore, suits all requirements of the case."

George Hagopian: In 1905, George Hagopian was ten years old when, he claimed, his uncle took him up Mount Ararat to see the Ark. He described "a great ship located on a rock ledge over a cliff and partially covered by snow." The vessel had a flat bottom and many windows along the top "big enough for a cow to walk through." He stood by his story for the rest of his life. Just before his death in 1972 his testimony was recorded and speech analysis indicated that he believed he was telling the truth.

Lieutenant Vladimir Roskovitsky: In the summer thaw of 1916 Lieutenant Vladimir Roskovitsky of the Russian Imperial Air Force reportedly spotted a half-submerged ship embedded in a frozen lake on the side of Mount Ararat during one of his high-altitude reconnaissance missions. He compared it in size to a modern battleship and he also described a large square doorway in the side of the vessel. He reported

Above: Mount Ararat, Turkey

his finding to the Tsar, who then allegedly sent an expedition to the site to photograph it and take measurements. They described "hundreds of small rooms" inside the Ark and "tiers of cages." They confirmed that the wood was "oleander, which belongs to the cypress family and never rots." After the Communist Revolution the following year, the trail goes cold, and all communications and photographs are untraceable. Maybe today they lie in a top secret Kremlin vault.

U.S. Air Force Europe Airplane: On June 17, 1949, an airplane crew photographed a dense, linear-shaped object and distinct "anomaly" protruding out from the "permanent glacial ice cap" at 15,500 feet at the very southwest edge of the nearly mile-long western plateau. They estimated its length at between 450 and 600 feet.

Fernand Navarra: In the summer of 1955, this French explorer and his twelve-year-old son climbed Mount Ararat and discovered hand-carved wooden beams embedded in the ice. Carbon-14 dating placed their age at a mere 2,000 years, but other methods such as wood-density analysis suggested they could be as much as 5,000 years old.

Turkish Air Force: In 1959, the crew of a Turkish airplane photographed a ship on the southern lower slopes of Mount Ararat, and, in 1960, it is alleged that the Turkish army exploded dynamite against the wall of the Ark, but found no evidence of cages or partitions inside.

CIA Reconnaissance Satellite: A CIA satellite took photographs of a purportedly "boat-like object" on Mount Ararat in September 1973.

Ron Wyatt and David Fasold: These two Ark hunters CAT-scanned the now buried vessel during the 1980s and concluded it was the Ark, after finding evidence of crisscrossed lines of iron.

A true legend?

An experienced Ararat guide, Dr. Ahmet Ali Arslan, believes "enough people have seen it (the Ark) within the last fifty or sixty years to establish the truth of the legend." However, the landscape, combined with its geopolitical location today, makes it virtually inaccessible.

PHILOSOPHER'S STONE

What is it?

Ancient alchemists used to believe that there was a mysterious unknown substance which would turn base metals into gold. They called it the "philosopher's stone."

Attempts to achieve this goal were called the "Great Work" or "Magnum Opus." Many hundreds of people throughout the centuries have attempted to concoct or discover this chemical substance.

Why a stone?

It isn't a stone as such, rather a substance. The meaning of the word "stone," in this context, is equivalent to the Latin *sub* and *stratus*, with the contained meaning that the experiment can *stand on it*. It is thus related to the cornerstone of a building, as well as a web of other related terms. Some believed it to be a red powder which would drive away the impurities of baser metals to leave pure gold.

What else did it represent?

Alchemists didn't just concern themselves with turning base metals into gold. The search for the philosopher's stone was a much bigger quest than this. As Lance S. Owens explains: "This simplification touches at only the most superficial veneer of alchemy . . . it had complex roots delving into the religious or philosophical subsoils of Western culture and aspirations far more subtle than the production of gold. Indeed, the dictum of medieval alchemists themselves avows this fact: *Aurum nostrum no est aurum vulgi* ('Our gold is not vulgar gold')."

The *Encyclopedia Britannica* describes the stone as "an elixir of life . . . the search for a method of upgrading less valuable metals but also of perfecting the human soul, the philosopher's stone was thought to cure illnesses, prolong life, and bring about spiritual revitalization."

Alchemy was metaphysical; science and spirit were inseparable—both sought to transform the dual nature of the soul toward perfection. It became a spiritual quest for the attainment of pure thought and spirit through strict devotional ritual and sanctity.

Where did the idea first appear?

The first mention is by a third-century Gnostic alchemist called Zosimos. He was captivated by the fact that "all things are woven together and all things are undone again; all things are mingled together and all things combine." He believed that "through the harmonies of separating and combining," anything within nature could be created, since "all things bring forth nature. For nature applied to nature transforms nature. Such is the order of natural law throughout the whole cosmos, and thus all things hang together."

Alchemy and Arabia

Between A.D. 300 and A.D. 1100, alchemy was the preserve of Arabia and its most renowned exponent, Jabir ibn-Hayyan, who was referred to by the European alchemists of later centuries as "Geber." He believed that if somehow the two most remarkable substances in nature—sulfur and mercury—could be combined together, with a binding agent or catalyst, then this would create gold.

Belief in this mysterious catalyst being a dry powder went back to the ancient Greeks, who called it *xerion*, from their word for "dry." The Arabs turned this into *al-iksir*, and the Europeans *elixir*. It was in Europe that it became known as the philosopher's stone, at a time when the word "philosopher" was synonymous with what we now call a "scientist."

For centuries the search for the philosopher's stone branched off into two quests: the one for gold and the other for eternal life.

Inventions and discoveries

Many early scientists have reached other inventions while searching for the philosopher's stone. *The Dictionary of Phrase and Fable* lists a few of these: "Boticher stumbled on the invention of Dresden porcelain manufacture; Roger Bacon on the composition of gunpowder; Geber on the properties of acids; Van Helmont on the nature of gas; and Dr. Glauber on the 'salts' which bear his name."

Where is it now?

The search for the philosopher's stone has never really gone away. It has changed over the centuries to suit the terminology and preoccupations of the time. In the twentieth century, it could be argued that it continued with the scientific quest for the Unifying Theory of Everything.

When Albert Einstein published his papers about the theory of relativity that led to the famous equation: $E=mc^2$, he needed to substitute an unknown quantity into his equations in order to construct his model of a static universe that could accommodate his theory of relativity without contracting under the force of gravity. So, to correct the error, he created a "cosmological constant." This doesn't seem a million miles away from this mysterious unknown substance that has always remained just out of reach.

PIRI REIS
MAP

What is it?

It is the earliest surviving map that shows the Americas. It was drawn on gazelle skin, with various colored illustrations and writings, 117 place-names, and thirty inscriptions. It is the only section of a larger world map, and it shows the western coast of Africa, the eastern coast of South America, and the northern coast of Antarctica.

However the Antarctic coastline, which is shown with incredible accuracy on the Piri Reis map, has been hidden by a layer of ice over a mile thick for the last 6,000 years. It means that before the invention of seismic profiling, the last time in human history that the coastline could have been plotted was 4000 B.C., when no one is supposed to have had either the naval technology or the mathematics to accomplish this remarkable feat.

Who made it?

It was drawn up in 1513 by a famous Turkish admiral, Piri Ibn Haji Mehmed ("Reis" means admiral). He admitted that he didn't survey the area himself, but merely compiled several other maps, some of which had been drawn up by his contemporaries, while others, he claimed, dated back to the fourth century B.C. or earlier.

His high rank in the navy meant that he was allowed privileged access to the Imperial Library of Constantinople, so he would certainly have been able to use a large number of source maps. Following a naval defeat against the Portuguese navy in the Red Sea in 1554, the sultan had him beheaded, and the map was lost for nearly 400 years.

Who found it?

In 1929 Mr. Halil Edhem, director of the National Museums in Turkey, discovered the map while sorting out the archives of the grandiose Ottoman Topkapi Serai Palace in Istanbul when the palace was being converted into a museum.

The Antarctic mystery

On the map, the northern coastline of Antarctica is perfectly drawn, despite the fact that it has been under ice since 4000 B.C. In 1966 Charles Hapgood's book *Maps of the Ancient Sea-Kings* brought this anomaly to the public attention and none other than Albert Einstein endorsed it and wrote in the foreword to the book, "His idea is original, of great simplicity, and—if it continues to prove itself—of great importance to everything that is related to the history of the earth's surface."

Hapgood claimed that the coastline details corresponded with the results of a seismic profile carried out by a Swedish-British Antarctic expedition of 1949. He argued that the ancient voyagers not only traveled from pole to pole, but also knew that the Earth was round, were able to work out longitude very accurately, and used complex spheroid trigonometry that supposedly wasn't known until the middle of the eighteenth century. In 1953 Arlington H. Mallery, an authority on ancient maps at the U.S. Navy Hydrographic Bureau, had examined the Piri Reis map and confirmed its accuracy by making a grid and transferring it onto a globe. He declared that it was a perfect match that should only have been possible with aerial surveying. Popular writer Erich von Däniken explained this by deciding that the map was the work of extraterrestrials.

However, Hapgood concluded the following: " . . . accurate information has been passed down from people to people. It appears that the charts must have originated with a people unknown and they were passed on, perhaps by the Minoans and the Phoenicians, who were, for a thousand years and more, the greatest sailors of the ancient world. We have evidence that they were collected and studied in the great library of Alexandria [Egypt] and that compilations of them were made by the geographers who worked there . . . Unbelievable as it may appear, the evidence nevertheless indicates that some ancient people explored Antarctica when its coasts were free of ice."

Still others believe that 4,000 years is too recent and that the ice may have covered the area as long ago as 9000 B.C. The riddle of the Piri Reis map is a long way from being solved.

ROSETTA STONE

What is it?

It is a slab of black granite dating from 196 B.C. inscribed by the ancient Egyptians with a royal decree praising their king Ptolemy V in the ninth year of his reign. It is three-feet nine-inches high, two-feet four-inches wide, and eleven inches thick, and it weighs three-quarters of a ton. The inscription is repeated three times, once in hieroglyphics, once in demotic (a cursive vernacular script developed late in Egyptian history), and once in Greek. Scholars have used the Rosetta Stone to unlock the mysteries of Egyptian hieroglyphics.

Who discovered it?

In 1799 it was none other than Napoleon and his troops who found it imbedded in a wall, which they demolished while digging the foundations for an extension to a fort near the seaside town of el-Rashid (Rosetta) in Egypt, 100 miles northwest of Cairo.

Who cracked the code?

Thomas Young, a British physicist and polymath, made the first groundbreaking steps while on holiday in Worthing, United Kingdom. He brought a copy of the Rosetta Stone inscriptions with him to pass the time and reasoned that cartouches (ovals drawn to contain a group of hieroglyphs) must refer to a name, which would be the same in all three languages. He successfully identified the word Ptolemy by comparing a cartouche with the Greek equivalent, but he didn't realize that this meant that the writing was phonetic—hieroglyphs corresponded to sounds.

It took Jean François Champollion, a French Egyptologist, to make this intellectual leap, which went against the thinking of the time. He was fluent in Coptic, a dead descendant of the ancient Egyptian language, having learned it as a teenager for theological study. Once he connected Coptic with the hieroglyphs he was able to find a phonetic representation of the ruler Ramesses. After weeks of study, he cracked the code and allegedly rushed into his brother's office exclaiming, "*Je tiens l'affaire!*" ("I've got it!"), after which he collapsed and was bedridden for the next five days.

This discovery has since enabled Egyptologists to read and understand all that remains of the Egyptians' ancient writings.

What does it say?

The inscription on the Rosetta Stone is a decree passed by the general council of Egyptian priests. The Ptolemies were Greeks who ruled Egypt after the fragmentation of Alexander the Great's empire. Prior to the issuing of the decree, there had been several years of insurgency in parts of the country which the Ptolemaic armies eventually crushed, but not without considerable effort. The decree, along with a coronation ceremony in Memphis, was intended to reunify Egypt by affirming the royal cult of this thirteen-year-old ruler throughout the country.

In English it runs to about 2,300 words and talks about Ptolemy's immortality and great benevolence, and details all the ways in which his people have prospered under divine leadership: "King Ptolemy, living forever, the Manifest God whose excellence is fine . . . he being a god, the son of a god and a goddess, and being like Horus son of Isis and

Osiris." It also stresses that "he has given much money and much grain to the temples of Egypt" and that he had established "peace in Egypt" and that he has brought prosperity to his people. It talks about his military conquests, the temples he has built, and the financial reforms and tax cuts he has instigated.

The final third of the writing instructs that a statue be built to him in every temple called "Ptolemy who has protected the Bright Land" and that "the priests should pay service to the statues in each temple three times a day, and they should lay down sacred objects before them and do for them the rest of the things that it is normal to do, in accordance with what is done for the other gods . . . "

Where is it now?

When Napoleon was defeated the Rosetta Stone became the property of the British, along with all the other antiquities that the French had discovered. Today it is on display at the British Museum in London, where it has been since 1802, apart from a brief period during the Second World War when it was moved, along with many other important artifacts, to a tunnel underneath Holborn underground station.

In July 2003 the Egyptians demanded the return of the Rosetta Stone. Dr. Zahi Hawass, secretary general of the Supreme Council of Antiquities in Cairo, issued a press release which said, "If the British want to be remembered, if they want to restore their reputation, they should volunteer to return the stone because it is the icon of our Egyptian identity."

SECRET TREASURES OF ZEUGMA

Where is it?

Zeugma was one of the great strategic fortress cities, comprised of two cities, Seleucia and Apamea, on either side of the Euphrates at the frontier of the Roman Empire. It is in southern Turkey close to its border with Syria.

In Roman times, Zeugma was the only place that had a permanent bridge across the River Euphrates, so it was a link between East and West and a critical trading center. Zeugma is Greek for "bridge." It was founded by one of Alexander the Great's generals, Seleucia Nicator, and it is a vitally important site for archaeologists and has the finest collection of Roman mosaics.

Unfortunately, this is an example of treasures lost in the last few years, entirely as a result of man. Since the building of the Birecik Dam, which was completed in 2001, most of the ancient city has been lost underneath its flood waters, despite the protestations of archaeologists who lobbied the Turkish government for a stay of execution to give them more time to excavate the site and recover some of its treasures before the flood waters buried them forever.

Above: *Statue of Mars, God of War*

What treasures did it contain?

Because of Zeugma's strategic position, it quickly became a large and wealthy place, and its inhabitants lived in great luxury. At one time it was twice the size of Roman London.

Archaeologists have long suspected Zeugma's importance, and this was confirmed in the late 1980s when Guillermo D. Algaze of the University of California at San Diego surveyed the area and discovered over forty places of historical significance. Many groups of archaeologists have excavated the site, including French archaeologists Pierre Leriche and Catherine Abadie-Reynal. The Turkish government was happy to accept such help from abroad, but no joint effort was made either to properly fund these teams or to prevent planning and the eventual construction of Birecik Dam.

In the summer of 2000, with time fast running out, archaeologists worked against the clock to uncover Zeugma's history, and at the eleventh hour, after years of under-funding and neglect, Zeugma's plight finally came to public attention with headline news. Unfortunately, it was too little too late. Construction of the dam was not halted, despite news that Catherine Abadie-Reynal had unearthed a masterpiece in the remains of a Roman villa: a spectacular mosaic floor, one of the finest examples ever discovered.

Then her team discovered yet more mosaics depicting a wide variety of mythological scenes and determined that Zeugma housed the largest collection of ancient mosaics anywhere in the world. The ones they could save were quickly dug out and removed from the villa and elsewhere, just days before the floodwaters turned the area into a vast lake. Many of these treasures are now in the nearby Gaziantep Museum.

The most spectacular mosaic depicted the gods Poseidon (god of the sea) and Oceanus and Tethys (two of the Titans). Evidence of a weaving industry was dug up, including loom weights and other weaving equipment; an ivory figurine of Aphrodite, goddess of love; a life-size bronze statue of Mars, god of war; and a host of other artifacts, many from the later Byzantine Era.

Fortunately, the treasures of Zeugma weren't only recovered during the last few years before the flooding; many mosaics and other items had been looted long ago and appear in museums all over the world, but it doesn't mitigate the fact that beneath the water lie treasures that are important not just for their beauty and craftsmanship, but for what they can teach us about life in Roman times.

SEVEN WONDERS OF THE ANCIENT WORLD

All seven of these magnificent constructions were famed throughout the ancient world and are remembered today as lost treasures of antiquity. Some inspired awe for their sheer size, others for their beauty, or both. All but one have long since disappeared, destroyed by time, looting, and natural disasters such as earthquakes and fire. If they were standing today, they would surely rival some of the great architectural and artistic achievements of the last 150 years.

Great Pyramid of Giza

The oldest and only one of the seven ancient wonders still surviving, it was built at the city of the dead, Giza, which is outside modern-day Cairo in Egypt. It was built by the Egyptian pharaoh Khufu around the year 2560 B.C. for his tomb and is thought to have taken twenty years to build.

Originally it was 481 feet high and had an outer casing that has since been pillaged, and it is now thirty feet shorter. It used two million blocks of stone, each weighing more than two tons, and it was the tallest man-made structure on the planet until the nineteenth century A.D. (apart from the fourteenth-century Gothic spire of Lincoln Cathedral in the UK which rose 525 feet, but collapsed in 1549). It was built with incredible accuracy, and the total error of the sloping angles is a mere one-tenth of a percent.

Hanging Gardens of Babylon

The Hanging Gardens were an elaborate complex of terraced gardens thought to have been built by Nebuchadnezzar II (604-562 B.C.) for his wife, Amyitis, to remind her of her green and mountainous homeland. The Greek historian Diodorus claimed the gardens were about 400 feet wide by 400 feet long and more than 80 feet high. They were located on the east bank of the River Euphrates, about thirty miles from Baghdad in modern Iraq. They used a chain pump irrigation system to lift millions of gallons of water from the nearby Euphrates River and were so spectacular that stories of their splendor were spread around the ancient world by travelers who claimed to have seen them.

Statue of Zeus at Olympia

At the ancient town of Olympia, on the west coast of modern Greece, about ninety miles west of Athens, stood the temple of Zeus. In 440 B.C. the Athenian sculptor Pheidias was instructed to begin work on an enormous statue of the seated god, made of wood, ivory, and gold. When complete, it was so huge that it looked as though he could dislodge the temple roof by standing up. The statue was forty feet high, the same as a four-story building today. Five hundred years later the Roman emperor Caligula tried to have it moved to Rome, but he failed when the scaffolding collapsed and killed his workmen. It was eventually transported to Constantinople, where it was destroyed by fire in A.D. 462.

Temple of Artemis at Ephesus

It was built around 550 B.C. in honor of the Greek goddess of hunting, on the orders of the Lydian king Croesus. Unusually, it was made of white marble and decorated inside with many statues and other works of art. It stood at Ephesus near the modern town of Izmir in Turkey. By all accounts it was a building of amazing beauty, 260 feet by 430 feet with 127 columns. It was destroyed on July 21, 356 B.C., when an arsonist called Herostratus sought to immortalize his name. Since this was the same day that Alexander the Great was born, the historian Plutarch reasoned that the goddess was "too busy taking care of the birth of Alexander to send help to her threatened temple."

Mausoleum at Helicarnassus

This was the magnificent burial place of Mausollos of Caria (hence mausoleum), renowned more for its beauty, decorations, and statues than its size, though that, too, was impressive. It stood in the city of Bodrum (Heliacarnassus) on the Aegean Sea, in southwest Turkey, and was completed around 350 B.C., three years after the king's death.

It remained intact for over 1,600 years, apart from a little earthquake damage, and might still stand today if it hadn't been for early-fifteenth-century crusaders, the Knights of Malta, who destroyed it and used its stones to build themselves a huge ugly castle.

Colossus of Rhodes

An enormous bronze statue of the sun god Helios erected in twelve years from 294 B.C., which, according to legend, bestrode the entrance of Mandraki harbor on the Mediterranean island of Rhodes in Greece. However, modern historians think it was probably situated on the eastern side of the harbor, or perhaps further inland.

It stood for just fifty-six years until it was toppled by an earthquake. The Egyptian Pharaoh Ptolemy III immediately offered to pay for its repair, but after consulting an oracle, the people of Rhodes decided to let it lie in ruin, where it remained for a further 900 years until the Arabs invaded Rhodes in A.D. 654 and sold it to a Syrian scrap-metal dealer. He broke it into pieces and took it back home on the backs of 900 camels.

Lighthouse of Alexandria

At 384 feet high it was the tallest building in the ancient world and stood on the island of Pharos, now a headland within the city of Alexandria in Egypt. It was commissioned by Alexander the Great's successor, Ptolemy Soter, around 290 B.C. but wasn't completed until after his death.

Its great mirror must have been a feat of ancient engineering, as its reflected light could be seen from thirty-five miles away. It was one of the most resilient of the ancient wonders, surviving an earthquake in A.D. 956. However, two more in the early fourteenth century must have inflicted severe damage, because by the time the famous Arab traveler Ibn Battuta visited it in 1349, it was too dangerous to enter. It hung on until A.D. 1480 when the Egyptian Mamelouk Sultan used its stones to build a medieval fort on top of its ruins.

SKULL OF
JOHN THE BAPTIST

Who was he?

John the Baptist was an apocalyptic visionary and the leader of an important ascetic movement in Galilee under Roman occupation in the first century A.D. He called upon his followers to confess their sins and renounce material comforts in preparation for the coming of the Messiah. He offered his ever-increasing peasant following baptism in the Jordan River, and baptized Jesus in this way.

How did he die?

He was arrested and imprisoned at Machaerus on the Dead Sea in A.D. 29 after he had denounced the incestuous marriage of the Roman ruler of Galilee, Herod Antipas, to his wife Herodias. At a banquet to celebrate Herod's birthday, his wife's daughter, Salome, danced for him and he offered to grant her anything she desired. At her mother's request, she demanded that the head of John the Baptist be brought to her on a platter.

What happened next?

According to Luke 8:3, Joanna, wife of Chuze and Herod's steward, recovered his head and buried it. It then spent several centuries changing hands, until it was taken to Bishop Ouranios of Cappadocia, in what is now central Turkey. In the ninth century it was taken to Constantinople (modern-day Istanbul). Since then many churches have claimed to have all or part of his skull or skeleton in their possession.

Amiens cathedral

This Knights Templar cathedral in Picardy, France, has the frontal part of the skull bearing a puncture mark just above the eye, said to have been made by Salome's knife after the head was presented to her. It was believed to have been brought there in A.D. 1206 by a canon named Wallon de Sarton who returned from the fourth Crusade and presented it to his bishop, Richard de Gerberoy. This immense Gothic cathedral was built to house the precious relic. Wallon claimed to have stolen the head from the Church of St. George in Constantinople. Theft of relics was common during this time, and known as *furtum sanctum*, or "holy theft." If a relic was stolen, it was seen as a sign that it had not been guarded closely enough and that Divine will had entrusted it into safer hands. From then on Amiens became a place of pilgrimage.

The Baphomet

The Knights Templar have been accused of worshipping an idol called Baphomet, which was believed to take the form of a head, the identity of which ranged from the Satanic goat head to the skull of John the Baptist. The Templars took part in the sacking of Constantinople in 1203, and Robert de Clari claimed that the head of John the Baptist was discovered at the Boucoleon Palace.

The search continues

The skull continues to make headlines, as every few years another archaeological team declares that they may have found the skull of John the Baptist.

In 1999 a team of archaeologists, digging underneath the remains of a fourth-century Byzantine church on the east bank of the Jordan River, discovered a cave carved in the first century A.D. Outside the cave they unearthed a human skull that had been buried separately, which some members of the team feel could belong to John the Baptist. The remains of three other ancient churches have been found in the area, confirming that it was a sacred site, and they are certain that the skull and cave belonged to a hermit. Project director Mohammad Waheeb reported, "Research has determined that the cave belonged to St. John the Baptist, but experts . . . are still examining the skull."

Another claim was made in 2002 when Israeli archaeologists were digging in the Qumran cemetery (near where the Dead Sea Scrolls were found—*see page 58*), where over 900 graves have been discovered dating to the time of a monastic sect called the Essenes. A skeleton and head were discovered in an elaborate burial chamber. Professor Richard Freund says that there is "circumstantial evidence" to suggest that the body belongs to John the Baptist and that he and the Essenes's spiritual leader, the "Teacher of Righteousness," were one and the same.

SODOM AND GOMORRAH

What are they?

The cities of Sodom and Gomorrah are now synonymous with their decadent inhabitants and their subsequent destruction by God. The demise of these two cities is described in the Old Testament. Archaeologists have long sought to find their ruins to prove they existed and to discover whether they really were destroyed by a cataclysmic event similar to the fire and brimstone raining from the sky that is described in the Bible.

Sodom and Gomorrah were two of five cities known as the Cities of the Plain. The other three were Zoar, Admah, and Zeboim.

Where are they?

For many years some scholars maintained that they didn't exist, largely based on the belief that there wasn't a route east of the Jordan River as described in the Bible. However, it was later proved that eastern travel was possible.

They have since been located on the east side of the Dead Sea in Jordan. At first it was thought that they were in the plain south of the Dead Sea and that the waters rose to cover them. In 1924 W. F. Albright, who had led an expedition to find the Cities of the Plain, reached this conclusion. But at a higher level just above the plain, he did find the ruins of a large fortress, Bad edh-Dhra, overlooking the ravine of Wadi Kerak, which he concluded was a point of pilgrimage during that time. He didn't realize he had discovered the lost city of Sodom.

During the 1960s and 1970s, the area was excavated again, and this time Bad edh-Dhra was found to have a twenty-three-foot-wide boundary wall that enclosed an area of about ten acres, and there was a large cemetery. Then the ruins of three more early-Bronze Age settlements were discovered overlooking the plain, dating from 3000 to 2000 B.C. Feifa was to the north of the first site, Numeira was to the south, and Safi between the two. When they discovered a fifth settlement, Khanazir, further south, they knew they had located the five Cities of the Plain.

How was it destroyed?

In Genesis 19:23-25 the destruction of the cities is described: "Then the Lord rained upon Sodom and upon Gomorrah brimstone and fire from the Lord out of heaven; And he overthrew those cities, and all the plain, and all the inhabitants of the cities, and that which grew upon the ground."

The area underground is rich in natural resources such as bitumen, petroleum, natural gas, and sulfur. Before the ruined cities were even discovered, scientist Frederick Clapp proposed the theory that an earthquake allowed combustible material to escape to the surface, whereupon it ignited, causing a massive fireball and throwing debris into the air, including bitumen and balls of sulfur (brimstone). There are major fault lines on either side of the Dead Sea, and the cities were built on the eastern fault line.

Much evidence has been found to support this theory; there is dark ash and charcoal covering the ruins at all of these sites. Paleoethnobotanists have studied seeds and irrigation systems to show that the populations of these cities were well fed and prosperous, and the types of graves and skeletal remains back this up. Their consumer culture was criticized in Luke 17:28: "[T]hey did eat, they drank, they bought, they sold, they planted, they builded."

The Bible also describes the disaster from Abraham's point of view. He was high up and to the west of the Dead Sea: "He looked down toward Sodom and Gomorrah, toward all the land of the plain, and he saw dense smoke rising from the land, like smoke from a furnace" (Genesis 19:28). Smoke from burning petroleum forced out of the ground under pressure would have sent up a plume of dense smoke in this way.

Bad edh-Dhra, the biggest site, was labeled as Sodom, and Numeira as Gomorrah. In Israel, to the southwest of the Dead Sea, is Mount Sodom, a geological ridge of pure salt seven miles long with many salt pillars, one of which is said to be Lot's wife, transformed into one of these bizarre formations when she disobeyed her husband and turned to look back on the destruction of Sodom and Gomorrah.

SPEAR OF
DESTINY

What is it?

The Spear of Destiny, also known as the Holy Lance and the Lance of
Longinus, is one of the three artifacts shrouded in mystery from Christ's
Passion, the others being the Holy Grail and the Crown of Thorns. The
legend of the spear comes originally from the book of John. According
to his account of the events at Golgotha, Jews asked the Roman soldiers
to break the legs of Jesus and the two men crucified with him. It could
take days to die on the cross; breaking the legs sped the process by
redistributing the weight and the Jews wanted the bodies to come down
before the Sabbath.

John wrote that one soldier, later identified as Gaius Cassius, and later
still called Longinus, used the spear to pierce Jesus' side to prove he was
already dead, therefore eliminating the need to break his legs.

According to John's account, blood and water flowed from the wound;
according to legend, some of the fluids splashed onto the soldier's eyes,
immediately repairing his failing vision.

What makes it so valuable?

Legend claims that whomever holds the spear has the power to control
the world. The holder is invincible—unless he loses the lance, in which

case he meets death almost immediately. The spear is said to have passed through the hands of world leaders throughout the ages including Herod the Great, Constantine, Justinian, Charlemagne, Otto the Great, Kaiser Wilhelm II of Germany, the Habsburg Emperors, and Adolf Hitler. Charlemagne is said to have carried the spear through 47 victorious battles, but died when he accidentally dropped it. At least one history attributed to the spear puts it in the hands of Frederick Barbarossa, who conquered Italy in the twelfth century. Barbarossa is said to have died minutes after accidentally dropping the spear into a stream.

Where is it?

There are four spearheads, none with the wooden shaft to which they were attached still in place. Each of the four have been said to be the Spear of Destiny. One is at the Vatican. Another is in Krakow, Poland, and a third is at Etschmiadzin in Armenia. But the lance most widely considered authentic resides in the Hofburg Museum in Vienna, Austria, where it is on public display.

The Vienna spear

The spear came into the House of the Habsburgs, and by 1912 was part of the collection at the Hofburg Museum. In September of that year, a young Adolf Hitler visited the museum and learned of the lance and its reputation. On March 14, 1938, Hitler annexed Austria and ordered that the spear—and the rest of the Habsburg collection—be sent to the city of Nuremberg. The spear was kept at St. Catherine's church for six years until 1944, when the collection was moved to an underground vault to protect it from Allied artillery and bombs. Allied forces invaded on April 30, 1945, taking possession of the vault—and the spear. A short while later that day, Hitler died by his own hand in a Berlin bunker.

After the war, the collection was returned to the museum, where it remains.

The other spears

One of the other spears was found by Peter Bartholomew in Antioch, Turkey, in 1098 during the Crusades. Under siege by Muslims at the time, the battle turned upon the spear's discovery, allowing the Christians to capture Antioch within a few days. That lance is now at Etschmiadzin in Armenia, but its origins have been questioned; some historians believe the artifact isn't the Roman lance at all, but the head of a Roman standard.

Another alleged Spear of Destiny has been in Krakow, Poland, since at least the 1200s. German records suggest, however, that the spear is a copy made from the German lance under Henry II, with a small sliver of the original embedded.

The final spear is said to be preserved at St. Peter's Basilica at the Vatican. It came into the posession of the Turks, and in 1492 the Sultan Bajazet sent it to Pope Innocent VIII to encourage him to keep the sultan's brother in prison. This lance has never since left Rome, although the Catholic Church makes no claims as to its authenticity as the Holy Lance.

THE SUNKEN CITY
OF HERAKLEION

How did archaeologists know Herakleion was lost?

Many classical writers have chronicled the life and times of Ancient Egypt's key harbor city of Herakleion, positioned at the Nile Delta on the Mediterranean coastline. Homer, Seneca, and Strabo bemoaned the loose morality of the citizens of Herakleion and the neighboring cities of Canopus and Menouthis. Herodotus described how Helena and her lover, Paris, were disappointed in their quest for refuge in Herakleion as they fled from the rage of her husband, Menelaus, king of the Spartans. Terrified of inducing Spartan rage, the people of Herakleion refused to harbor the couple, who then headed to Troy. Following Menelaus's recapture of his wife, Herodotus described the two resting in Herakleion.

But more than 1,000 years ago, in the eighth century, scientists speculate that a massive earthquake in the Mediterranean caused a tsunami that engulfed the three cities and sent them to the seabed.

How was the sunken city discovered?

In 1996 a team of scientists began the arduous task of surveying 100 square miles of the Mediterranean Sea, searching for geophysical evidence that would lead them to the discovery of Herakleion. The team of geophysicists, marine archaeologists, divers, and historians was headed

Above: A marine archaeologist inspects an ancient wall

by French marine archaeologist Franck Goddio. It was a two-year labor of love that finally paid off when the silt-covered ruins of the city were found, ten miles off the Egyptian coast, in the bay of Abukir, sixty feet below the surface of the sea. They had uncovered a sunken treasure trove, covering an area of the seabed 3,250 feet long and 2,600 feet wide.

The team's sophisticated electronic equipment also helped to clarify what had sent the city beneath the waves: they pinpointed a seismic fault running straight through the middle of the site. Evidence indicated that Herakleion had been inhabited continuously since 1500 B.C. But in a moment, a vast natural disaster had sunk the so-called "city of sin" to the bottom of the Mediterranean. Nearby Alexandria has much archaeological and historical evidence of several shattering earthquakes.

What was recovered from the site?

Herakleion has yielded a vast treasure from its watery grave. Houses, temples, a coliseum, and the battered remains of a fleet of at least ten ships in a complex infrastructure that once formed the harbor have been identified. The positioning of the wrecked fleet is sensational, as it offers an unprecedented opportunity to examine an ancient harbor, but also indicates the speed with which the city must have been overcome. The wrecks of the ten or more ships add credence to the theory that a giant tidal wave, a tsunami, was responsible for the cataclysm.

The temple area is full of bronze, gold, and bejeweled artifacts, and three colossal pink granite statues, two of an unidentified pharaoh and queen, and the third of the Nile god of flooding, Hâpi. Several more exquisite statues were also recovered at the temple site, all of which have been dated as being no older than the first century.

Perhaps the most dramatic find of all was the discovery of a black granite pillar, inscribed with hieroglyphs that tell of an edict, issued by the pharaoh Nektanebos I, that instated a compulsory ten percent tax on all Greek imports in order to help fund the building of the temple to the goddess Neith. The edict specifies that the pillar was to be erected in the town of Herakleion. Here, then, was the final confirmation that the sunken ruins were, indeed, the lost city of Herakleion.

IVBA REX.

REX. IVBA

Apud Fuluium Vrsinum in nomismate argenteo.

TREASURE OF KING JUBA

What is it?

In 1982, an amateur treasure hunter, Russell E. Burrows, found a remote cave near his hometown of Olney in southern Illinois. After advancing through a 500-foot-long tunnel lined with oil lamps, he discovered several chambers filled with ancient weapons, gold sarcophagi, jewels, and stone tablets depicting Roman soldiers, Jews, early Christians, and West African sailors. He removed more than 7,000 artifacts from the cave and then sealed the entrance using dynamite, following the controversy over his discovery.

The case for the treasure's origins is argued in Frank Joseph's controversial book, *The Lost Treasure of King Juba: The Evidence of Africans in America before Columbus*.

Who was King Juba II?

Juba's father was king of Numidia (modern-day northeast Libya) on the North African coast. He fought with Pompey against Julius Caesar and the Roman Empire in 46 B.C. After they were defeated, Juba's father committed suicide rather than allow himself to be taken alive, and his baby son, Juba II, was taken back to Rome by Caesar as a trophy.

Juba was brought up as a Roman by Caesar's nephew Octavian. He was well educated and became one of the most learned men of his day. When Octavian became emperor, he installed Juba as ruler of Mauritania on the West Coast of Africa. He later married Cleopatra Selene, the daughter of Antony and Cleopatra, and together they ruled from 25 B.C. to around A.D. 19.

They turned their kingdom into a cultured and prosperous land and introduced Greek architecture and art to North Africa. Juba continued with his academic and field studies, writing histories of Africa and Arabia and even corresponding with Pliny the Elder about botany and zoology. He is credited with discovering a succulent plant, which he named *Euphorbia* in honor of his family physician, Euphorbus.

How did Juba end up in North America?

According to Frank Joseph, Juba was persecuted by the Emperor Caligula and his son Ptolemy was executed, causing a Mauritian rebellion against the Romans. They moved southeast into present-day Ghana, built a fleet of ships, and set sail to establish their kingdom on another continent. They made off with Cleopatra's treasure and King Juba's library.

Why Illinois?

Russell E. Burrows is the only person who knows where the treasure was found and yet Frank Joseph claims that the hoard is proof that Africans reached America long before Columbus.

Unfortunately the book doesn't argue a convincing case. According to Sarah Meador, writing for Rambles.net, an online cultural arts magazine, some of the book is "laughably melodramatic and poorly researched" and "every scrap of obscure artistic knowledge possible is brought to bear on numerous illustrations of the surviving artifacts . . . the research is brief and repetitive. Most of Joseph's historic information is based on extremely outdated history texts."

She says she hopes that the book is a hoax since, if it really is the lost treasure of Juba, most of the artifacts have been melted down and sold, representing "the greatest loss to archaeology since the days of using mummies as engine fuel."

But there's an even more obvious problem: why Illinois? Why didn't Juba settle further east in North Carolina or Virginia? Why did he travel so far inland? And why do so many people still believe that Juba II and Cleopatra Selene are buried in Kubr-er-Rumia (Tombeau de la Chretienne) in Algeria?

Is it a hoax?

The gold artifacts look crude, and archaeologists and linguists have disputed the authenticity of the stone inscriptions. Nevertheless there is evidence that Burrows may have found an archaeological site of great value and taken drastic steps to preserve his claim to it.

In the decades since he announced his discovery, the bitter arguments over Burrows's cave have not abated. Critics who dismiss it as a hoax are still debated vigorously by those who believe the gold Burrows recovered is proof that Africans visited the shores of North America more than fifteen centuries before Columbus. The only thing that can be said with any certainty is that the controversy surrounding King Juba's gold will only add to its mystery.

TREASURE OF
SUTTON HOO

What is it?

In the seventh century A.D., a king was buried near the River Deben in Woodbridge in southeast Suffolk, England. There are several other burial mounds on the site, but in 1939 when archaeologists excavated the largest of them, they discovered a wooden ship laden with treasure. It is unusual because ship burials in England were rare and its hoard of magnificent artifacts makes it the most significant archaeological find ever in Britain.

Who discovered it?

In the late 1930s, Edith May Pretty was living at Sutton Hoo House and the burial mound was located on her estate. Following a vivid dream that convinced her that there was treasure beneath the largest mound (others say she saw a vision of an armed warrior standing on the mound at dusk), she wrote to the Ipswich Museum asking them to send an expert to survey the site. She was provided with local archaeologist Basil Brown. Daunted by the size of mound one, he explored some of the smaller ones, and he didn't tackle the largest mound until May of the following year. An exploratory side trench soon revealed iron rivets, and, realizing he had discovered an unlooted ship burial, he closed the trench and began digging from the top of the mound, so that he could uncover the vessel where it lay.

What treasure was buried in the ship?

The magnificent wooden ship was almost ninety feet long and fifteen feet wide and would have housed at least forty rowers. All the burial objects had been placed inside the ship (the body had completely decayed because of the high acidity of the soil, although phosphate residues make it likely that there was once a body there, and the mound wasn't just a cenotaph).

The most famous artifact is the helmet, which has become a symbol of the discovery. When it was found it was in hundreds of fragments, which were painstakingly reconstructed at the British Museum. It was made from a single piece of iron and it had ear and neck guards attached as well as other decorative features. The helmet was decorated with bronze mythological scenes and animal motifs and inlaid with silver wire.

The king's sword and shield were in much worse condition. The wood and leather shield has been reconstructed and the original ornate metal fixings have been attached, including a bird of prey and a dragon. The sword was a sophisticated piece of work for the time; it was pattern welded from fifty-six plaited iron rods to form a distinctive herringbone pattern and it had a carbon-steel cutting edge. The components which made up the sword handle were exquisite and of the highest craftsmanship.

The other objects were a mixture of the local and the exotic. There is a hanging bowl with red roundels decorated with Celtic swirls—a typical piece from the Celtic Iron Age, whereas a set of eight silver bowls originated from the Byzantine world.

Some of the smaller pieces have elaborate gold decorations and are of a level of craftsmanship unparalleled in Europe at the time. These include a purse with an ornate lid that contained thirty-seven gold coins dated to A.D. 625. There is a sword belt and scabbard. One of the most impressive smaller pieces is an intricate gold buckle made from 14.8 ounces of cast gold; it is hollow and hinged and has an ingenious locking mechanism.

There were also sumptuous feasting objects such as silver plates, wooden cups and bottles, and two large drinking horns.

Which king was buried there?

Most historians agree that the grave belonged to King Rædwald, who ruled Britain after he defeated Æthelfrith, King of Northumbria, at the Battle of the River Idle around A.D. 617, and who died around A.D. 625.

Where is it now?

A coroner's inquest decreed that the ship and its treasure did not belong to the Crown, since it had not been lost, but deliberately buried and abandoned. Ownership was therefore granted to the landowner, Edith May Pretty. However, she donated it to the state and now the collection is housed in the British Museum.

TROY AND
ITS TREASURE

What is it?

Troy is an ancient city in Turkey near the Dardanelles. In the Bronze Age it was a Phrygian settlement and later became the legendary city of the Trojan War when it was captured and sacked by the Greeks around 1200 B.C.

Who found it?

Heinrich Schliemann located Troy by looking for clues in Homer's *Iliad*. He dug in partnership with Englishman Frank Calvert, but they fell out over working practices, so it is Schliemann's name that lives on today.

He was born in 1822 in Germany, and during his childhood his reading of Homer's epic account of the Trojan War gave him a life-long fascination for the lost city. When he was nine years old, he and his childhood sweetheart, Minna Meincke, pledged that one day they would first excavate the ruins of a nearby castle to locate the lost gold of the robber baron Henning Von Holstein, then use this to fund a grand expedition to Asia Minor to discover Troy. Circumstances prevented him from staying in contact with Minna, but he never lost sight of his life's ambition.

However, Schliemann was a retired millionaire in his late forties when he finally turned all his attention to locating Troy and began excavating the site in 1871. During his eventful life he had taught himself several

European languages, and became a rich man trading in Russia and later dealing Californian gold. He had also spent the previous two years in Paris studying archaeology.

Where is it?

While many historians considered Troy to be fictional, the prevailing opinion among those who believed that Troy was real was that it was situated on a hill called *Bunarbashi*. Schliemann felt that its aspect and location did not tally with Homer's description in the *Iliad*. It mentioned that Mount Ida was visible from Troy—from *Bunarbashi* it was not; the city should have been closer to the sea, about four miles closer by Schliemann's calculations. Furthermore, Homer describes how the Greek warrior Achilles pursued Hector around the city walls—one of the sides of the hill was too steep for this to have been possible. Schliemann tried it himself and concluded, "I needed almost a quarter of an hour to get to the bottom. I then became convinced that no mortal, not even a goat, would have been able to descend in a speedy trot."

Schliemann decided that the most likely candidate was another hill near the village of Hissarlik, which fulfilled all the Homeric criteria that *Bunarbashi* lacked. He wasn't alone in his suspicions: fifty years earlier Charles Maclaren had written his *Dissertation on the Topography of the Plain of Troy*, naming the same location; also Frank Calvert, with whom Schliemann entered into a digging partnership, suspected the site. However, their temperaments were very different. When they discovered not one but eleven Troys, each one built on the ruins of those beneath, Schliemann ignored the advice of the more cautious Calvert, and hacked down to the level which he believed was the real Troy, the second from the bottom, destroying all the archaeology from all the other layers. The two men fell out but Schliemann continued undeterred.

Which is the real Troy?

Of the eleven strata, Schliemann believed that the second to the bottom one was Troy because it showed signs of having been burned down (as described in the *Iliad*). However, dating methods proved that this level was too ancient; Wilhelm Dorpfeld, one of Schliemann's assistants, believed that Troy VI was the Homeric Troy; though later changed his mind to Troy VII.

What treasure did he find?

On May 31, 1873, Schliemann found a copper jug embedded in a shaft wall. He sent all his workers on a break and dug out a hoard of treasure which included golden earrings, pots of silver and gold, and two royal diadems each composed of 16,000 individual pieces of gold, woven together with gold threading. He kept his findings a secret and later smuggled them out of the country, much to the anger of the Turkish government, who sued him for their return. Schliemann paid five times the eventual court settlement so that he could gain permission to re-enter the country to resume digging. He named his hoard the "Treasure of Priam."

His hasty methods have been criticized, and he has been accused of faking artifacts and embellishing stories, but his discoveries brought him worldwide fame and led some to hail him as an archaeological genius.

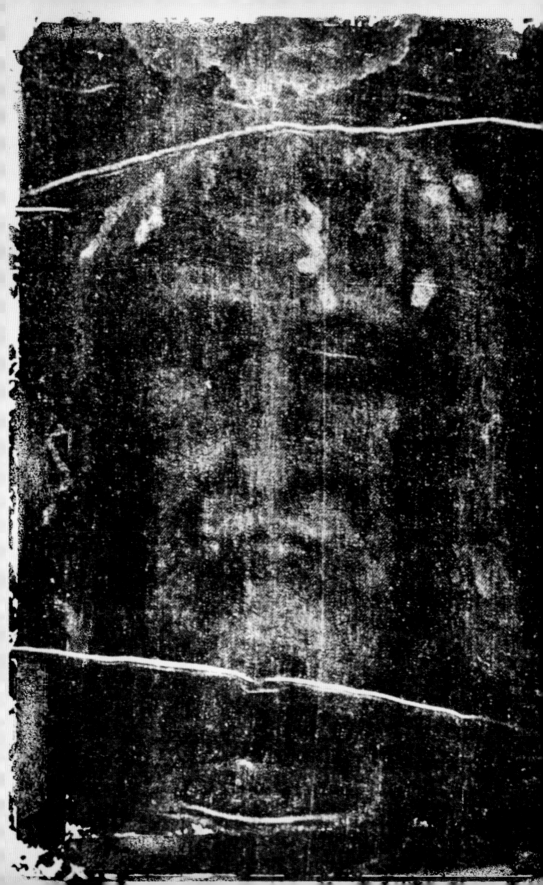

TURIN
SHROUD

What is it?

It is a linen cloth, fourteen feet long, that bears the image of a crucified man. It is the most studied artifact in human history. Many believe it is the burial shroud of Jesus of Nazareth. It contains human blood and wounds consistent with His crucifixion as described in the Bible: crown of thorns, bruising of face, scourge marks, nail wounds to wrist and feet, wound in side. The miracle is taken as a sign that the resurrection really happened and that Jesus was divine.

How old is it?

The shroud's fully documented history began in Western Europe when it was revealed by Geoffrey DeCharney in Lirey, France, in 1353. In 1578 it was moved to Turin, Italy, for safekeeping, where it remains to this day.

In 1988, carbon-14 (C14) testing concluded that it was 600 years old, but the protocol that was followed during this test has since been called into question. Only one sample of cloth was used (instead of three) and this was taken from an outside edge, which had been extensively handled for centuries, was close to water damage and a scorch mark, and may have been a piece of fabric used to repair the shroud. It was badly damaged by fire in 1532. All of these factors could affect the dating result.

The images of two coins placed over the eyes consistent with Jewish burial customs match those minted in A.D. 29-33 during the reign of Pontius Pilate.

Textile analysis reveals that the cloth was hand-woven before the twelfth century, is of Middle Eastern origin, and measures exactly two by eight Syrian cubits, a Middle East shroud measurement. The cloth contains particles of limestone indigenous to caves surrounding Jerusalem.

Real or fake?

Over the years a number of tests have been used to establish its origins:

Heat scorch: If the image was somehow scorched onto the linen, it would glow under ultraviolet light (as do the scorch marks from 1532). It does not.

X-rays: Giles Carter, a shroud researcher, suggests that the body emitted X-rays. He has detected X-ray imagery in the mouth and finger (teeth and carpal bones).

Painted forgery: Many tests, including infrared light spectrometry and microscopic viewing, have proved conclusively that it was not painted. The image is present only within the very topmost fibers and there is no evidence of capillary action. There is no image below any of the blood stains. There is no significant trace of ink, dye, or pigment.

Photographic image: Is it possible that someone discovered a photographic process centuries earlier than officially documented? Leonardo da Vinci described a camera obscura (pinhole camera) in his notebooks, but there is no trace of photographic chemicals (e.g. silver nitrate) on the linen.

Body amines reacting with starch: A faint image of a second face was recently discovered on the back of the cloth. It supports the hypothesis that is growing in popularity that superficial carbon bonds (the microscopic pixels which make up the image) are the result of a reaction between body amines (ammonia derivates) and a thin layer of starch on the fibers used in the weaving process (starch was used to make the fibers weave smoothly and prevent snagging). The image corresponds to a mathematical gradient related to distance between body and cloth. According to Dr. John Jackson, this is "confirmation that the Shroud covered a body shape at the time of image formation."

Where is it now?

The shroud is kept in the cathedral of St. John the Baptist in Turin, Italy.

TUTANKHAMUN

Who was King Tutankhamun?

Egyptian pharaoh Tutankhamun, or King Tut as he's become known, ruled from about 1334–1325 B.C. Ascending to the throne at age nine as the twelfth ruler of Egypt's eighteenth dynasty, Tutankhamun was not considered a significant leader. It is likely that his obscurity caused his tomb to be forgotten by most, allowing it to remain mostly intact until its discovery in 1922.

Because Tutankhamun was relatively unknown and ruled only nine years until his death at age eighteen, few details of his life are known. Scholars surmise he was the son of Akhenaten, known as the heretic pharaoh, and Kiya. There is some evidence that he was married at age nine to his half sister, Ankhesenpaaten. Historians suspect Ankhesenpaaten was older then Tutankhamun because she was probably of child-bearing age as it appears she already had a child by her father, Akhenaten. Although there is no record to suggest Tutankhamun was survived by any off-spring, a pair of mummified, premature fetuses was found in his tomb, suggesting he fathered two children who perished at birth.

Where is Tutankhamun's tomb?

King Tut's tomb is in Egypt's Valley of the Kings on the west bank of the Nile River. It is near the city now known as Luxor, formerly Thebes, 313 miles south of Cairo.

Who found it?

English Egyptologist Howard Carter gained the financial backing of Lord Carnarvon, an amateur archaeologist, in 1907. Carter had been working in Egypt since 1891, when he was seventeen years old. Although World War I brought their work to a virtual standstill, they began excavating in the Valley of the Kings in earnest in 1917. Carter found evidence that Tutankhamun's tomb was nearby, uncovering a piece of gold foil, a faience cup, and an array of funerary items that bore the pharaoh's name. Yet, by 1921 Carter had found little of substance and Lord Carnarvon was growing tired of financing the project. After some discussion, the two men agreed to one final season of searching.

On November 4, 1922, Carter uncovered a step; by the next day, his crew had excavated twelve steps leading downward to the upper portion of a sealed door, clearly of eighteenth dynasty design. Excited, Carter sent for Lord Carnarvon. He arrived on November 23 and work continued.

It was clear that grave robbers had entered the tomb at least twice, probably more than 3,000 years earlier. But their path had been through small holes, allowing them to carry out only the smallest of items. Digging through limestone chips used to fill a twenty-six-foot-long passageway, it took Carter's team several days to reach the outer chamber of the tomb. At long last, Carter was able to peek inside.

He wrote: "I was struck dumb with amazement, and when Lord Carnarvon, unable to stand the suspense any longer, inquired anxiously, 'Can you see anything?' it was all I could do to get out the words, 'Yes, wonderful things.'"

What was in King Tut's tomb?

Carter found the antechamber of the tomb filled to the ceiling with artifacts—boxes, chairs, couches, and other items—and almost all of it gold. It took seven weeks to remove the treasure.

On February 17, 1923, Carter was ready to move beyond the antechamber. Cautiously peering into the next room with a flashlight, he found an even larger cache. As Carter described it, "I inserted an electric torch. An astonishing sight its light revealed, for there, within a yard of the doorway, stretching as far as one could see and blocking the entrance to the chamber, stood what to all appearances was a solid wall of gold . . . "

Eventually inside the burial chamber, Carter's team found four shrines made of gilded wood, the largest more than sixteen feet long, ten feet wide, and nine feet tall, each section of the shrine weighing as much as 1,000 pounds. Inside the fourth shrine they discovered Tutankhamun's yellow sarcophagus, made from a single piece of quartzite. When they raised the 2,500-pound lid from the stone box, they found the boy king's mummified body inside the innermost of three coffins.

Inside, King Tut had lain covered by a magnificent burnished gold mask for 3,300 years.

In all, Carter's team withdrew more than 3,000 items from the tomb, a process that took ten years. At least 150 items were found on the mummy alone, almost all of them gold.

The ancient Egyptians believed that if a person's name lived on, so did their soul. Thanks to Howard Carter, Tutankhamun may live forever.

VEIL OF VERONICA

What is it?

The controversial Turin Shroud (*see page 188*), which believers argue was the burial cloth of Jesus Christ, is not the only holy relic in the possession of the Roman Catholic Church that is said to depict the image of Christ's face.

The Veil of Veronica is a heavily guarded, less-well-publicized treasure. It is a very thin piece of linen, measuring only 6.7 by 9.4 inches, and bears, in reddish-brown, the unmistakable image of the face of a bearded, longhaired man with open eyes. The signs of suffering are clear: the face looks tired, bruised, and scarred, and there are blood spots around the forehead and nose.

Why is it so special?

According to Christian legend, Veronica was so moved when she saw Jesus struggling under the weight of the cross he had to carry through Jerusalem, she stepped forward to wipe blood and sweat from his face. Her kindness was repaid with a miracle: the image of Christ's face was perfectly imprinted in her veil. The story of the miracle forms part of the Catholic Lenten prayers called the Stations of the Cross, and Veronica is a saint.

The veil is said to have healing powers. Veronica offered the veil to the Emperor Tiberius, who supposedly recovered from a terrible sickness after gazing at the image. From then on Veronica left the veil in the care of the Vatican, with Pope Clement, the fourth pope.

Where is it now?

The exact whereabouts of the Veil of Veronica today are the subject of some contention. For centuries the Vatican has listed the veil as one of its holy relics, and a Latin inscription on the figure of Veronica beside the main altar in St. Peter's Basilica in Rome testifies to this, saying the veil lies within the statue.

However, in May 1999, a German Jesuit priest, Father Heinrich Pfeiffer, announced that he had identified the true veil in a small Capuchin friary, the Sanctuary of the Sacred Face, in the small town of Manoppello in Italy's Apennine Mountains. Pfeiffer's announcement, the result of thirteen years of study into the veil, was met by the Vatican with a marked silence. He claims that it was stolen from the Vatican in the early seventeenth century, and he points to records showing that the chapel where Veronica's Veil was originally kept was demolished in 1608 during a major restoration program at St. Peter's. Pfeiffer contends that the theft of the relic would have been easy amid the chaos of the restoration. Interestingly, he has discovered references to the veil in the records from the Sanctuary of the Sacred Face friary dating to about the same time.

Vatican records from 1616 illustrate that the veil was a much-copied relic. Pfeiffer suggests that the Vatican holds one such copy today. In 1618 a Vatican archivist catalogued all objects in the old Basilica and referred to the broken glass on the reliquary that contained Veronica's Veil. Pfeiffer's examination of the veil in Manoppello revealed a fragment of glass on the edge of the fabric.

Pfeiffer's theories are further supported by a 1646 account written by a Capuchin friar named Donato da Bomba, in which a woman named Marzia Leonelli is said to have sold the veil in 1608 to post bail to release her husband from jail. The veil was said to have been part of her dowry. As the relic was in poor condition, it was donated to the friary thirty years later.

Is the image miraculous?

At first sight, many who have seen the almost transparent cloth say the image is merely a painting. But tests have proved conclusively that there is no paint or dye detectable on the cloth, nor have colored threads been used to weave the image. Certainly, it bears the appearance of blood, but further testing is needed to find the origins of the marks.

The image is only visible in certain lights; sometimes it is completely invisible. This in itself would have been considered miraculous in the Middle Ages, when no painting technique could possibly have produced such an effect. Another curious feature of the image is that it is identical on both sides of the cloth. It is not possible to reproduce an identical image on the reverse with medieval painting techniques. The precision-match of the image on the reverse compares to a modern photographic plate. Indeed, only highly sophisticated modern digital photographic technology, carried out at the Gregorian University, has enabled the match to be measured and confirmed as identical.

The most astounding part of this whole mystery is that when the Holy Shroud of Turin is superimposed over the Veil of Veronica, the faces are an identical match, adding further weight to the theory that they belong to the same man.

Of course there are many skeptics in the academic community. Keith Ward, regius professor of divinity at Oxford University, has been quoted as saying, "The Gregorian University is quite respectable, but I think the claim about the veil is totally absurd. Almost everybody accepts it as legend. I'd put it on the same level as seeing the face of Mohammed in a potato." Pfeiffer remains undeterred: "Yes I am convinced . . . this is the famous relic."

YAMASHITA'S GOLD

What is it?

Yamashita's gold is a secret hoard of gold, priceless art, and religious artifacts looted by the Japanese from their Asian colonies during World War II, which has never been recovered. Legend has it that Emperor Hirohito ordered the loot to be hidden in underground caverns built into the mountainsides of the Philippines during the war, as the Pacific War made shipping it into Japan too risky. General Tomoyuki Yamashita was the Japanese general in charge of the Philippines, and it has been alleged that he must have been the ringleader of the operation.

How was it hidden?

The loot is purported to have been hidden in over 100 different sites in the Philippines, but the focus for treasure hunters is predominantly in the mountains of Luzon. Many stories circulate about how these tunnels and caverns were constructed.

Prisoners of war were said to have been used in many cases, and then they were sealed in with the treasure by blasts of dynamite so they couldn't divulge its secret location. In their book *Gold Warriors*, Sterling and Peggy Seagrave say that the engineers used in the operation were invited to attend a party to mark the end of the operation, days before American tanks closed in on them. The tunnel where the party was held, stacked high with rows of gold bullion, was to become their tomb, as dynamite charges were set off at midnight, the imperial princes having first made their escape along with General Yamashita. Yamashita surrendered to the Americans three months later and was subsequently tried and executed for war crimes.

What happened to the gold?

The official line is that it has never been recovered, and moreover, that the story is considered by most to be little more than urban myth. However, this is by no means the full story.

Many treasure hunters have risked their life savings and, in some cases, their lives trying to locate the loot. In the city of General Santos, two Filipinos were buried alive when the tunnel they had been digging collapsed. Many former Japanese soldiers who claim to have been witnesses to the operation are among those prepared to take these risks. The wife of the former president of the Philippines, Imelda Marcos, claimed that much of her husband's wealth originated from a substantial hoard of Yamashita's gold. Skeptics dismiss this as a weak attempt to hide the real source—his embezzlement from the national treasury.

Fighting Communism

Sterling and Peggy Seagrave's theory is among the most intricate and controversial of all. They claim that the United States, under President Harry Truman, confiscated a substantial stash of gold bullion found on the Philippines after the end of the war. Truman, they allege, decided that the gold should remain a state secret, and it was held in bank accounts all over the world, along with Nazi plunder (see page 126). The "black gold" became known as "The Black Eagle Trust," and has been used ever since, claim the Seagraves, as an undeclared fund with which the United States has helped fight Communism and bolster anti-Communist nations. Furthermore, Truman's plan necessitated a non-Communist ally in Asia, and it was in his interests not to blame Japan publicly for plundering treasure from its Asian colonies. They contend that the United States has systematically refused to grant any claim for compensation made against Japan with respect to the Second World War ever since.

The theory makes for an interesting read, but fails to convince skeptics, who point out that there has been no convincing historical evidence to support the existence of the gold. They also draw attention to the fact that Yamashita was never given any particular favor by the leading lights in the Japanese military; to be endowed with such a substantial responsibility would have been highly unlikely. He took up his post in the Philippines in December 1944. Before he surrendered in September 1945, U.S. air, land, and sea forces caused so much chaos on the islands that Yamashita would have been preoccupied with relocating his headquarters, something he was forced to repeat at least six times. This time-consuming and highly pressured activity makes the construction of miles of underground, highly inaccessible tunnels and the movement of billions of dollars worth of gold even less plausible.

Nevertheless, the legend of Yamashita's gold continues to perplex treasure hunters and those seeking war reparations and justice.

RECOMMENDED READING

The Amber Room: The Controversial Truth about the Greatest Hoax of the Twentieth Century
Catherine Scott-Clark and Adrian Levy, Atlantic Books, 2005.

America's Lost Treasure
Tommy Thompson, Atlantic Monthly Press, 1998.

Atlantis: The Antediluvian World
Ignatius Donnelly, Dover Publications, 1976.

The Bronze Age Computer Disc
Alan Butler, Foulsham, 1999.

The Complete Dead Sea Scrolls in English: Complete Edition (Penguin Classics)
Geza Vermes, Penguin Books, 2004.

The Complete Tutankhamun: The King, the Tomb, the Royal Treasure
Seventh Earl of Carnarvon, Thames and Hudson, 1995.

The Copper Scroll Decoded: One Man's Search for the Fabulous Treasure of Ancient Egypt
Robert Feather, Thorsons, 1999.

The Crystal Skull
Richard M. Garvin, Simon & Schuster, 1974.

Danger, My Ally: The Amazing Life Story of the Discoverer of the Crystal Skull
F. Mitchell-Hedges, Adventures Unlimited Press, 1995.

The Dead Sea Scrolls Deception
Michael Baigent and Richard Leigh, Random House of Canada, 2001.

Divine Spark of Creation: The Crystal Skull Speaks
Kathleen Murray, Galactic Publications, 1998.

Edgar Cayce on Atlantis
Edgar Cayce, Little, Brown and Company, 2000.

Edgar Cayce's Atlantis and Lemuria: The Lost Civilizations in the Light of Modern Discoveries
Frank Joseph, A.R.E. Press, 2001.

Fatal Treasure: Greed and Death, Emeralds and Gold, and the Obsessive Search for the Legendary Ghost Galleon Atocha
Jedwin Smith, John Wiley & Sons, 2005.

Forbidden Archaeology: The Hidden History of the Human Race
Michael A. Cremo and Richard L. Thompson, Bhaktivedanta Book Trust, 2001.

From the Omens of Babylon: Astrology and Ancient Mesopotamia
Michael Baigent, Arkana, 1994.

The Genesis Flood
Henry M. Morris, J C Whitcomb, P & R Publishing Co, Baker Pub Group, 1989.

Gold Warriors: America's Secret Recovery of Yamashita's Treasure
Sterling Seagrave and Peggy Seagrave, Verso Books, 2003.

A Guide Book of Double Eagle Gold Coins: A Complete History and Price Guide
Q. David Bowers, Whitman Publishing, 2004.

Heaven's Mirror: Quest for the Lost Civilization
Graham Hancock, Crown Publishers, 1998.

Hitler's Silent Partners: Swiss Banks, Nazi Gold, and the Pursuit of Justice
Isabel Vincent, William Morrow, 1997.

Holy Blood, Holy Grail
Michael Baigent, Richard Leigh, and Henry Lincoln, Delacorte Press, 2004.

Holy Grail: Imagination and Belief
Richard Barber, Harvard University Press, 2004.

The Iliad (Oxford World's Classics)
Homer, Oxford University Press, 2004.

Illegal Tender: Gold, Greed, and the Mystery of the Lost 1933 Double Eagle
David Tripp, Simon & Schuster, 2004.

In Search of King Solomon's Mines
Tahir Shah, Arcade Publishing, 2003.

Investigating the Unexplained: Compendium of Mysteries of the Natural World
Ivan T. Sanderson, Prentice Hall, 1972.

King Solomon's Mines (Oxford World's Classics)
H. Rider Haggard, Oxford Paperbacks, 1998.

The Lost Dutchman Mine of Jacob Waltz: The Golden Dream
Thomas E. Glover, Cowboy Miner Productions, 2001.

Lost Secrets of the Sacred Ark: Amazing Revelations of the Incredible Power of Gold
Laurence Gardner, HarperCollins, 2003.

Lost Ship of Noah
Charles Berlitz, WH Allen, 1988.

The Lost Treasure of King Juba: The Evidence of Africans in America Before Columbus
Frank Joseph, Bear & Company, 2003.

Lost Treasure of the Knights Templar: Solving the Oak Island Mystery
Steven Sora, Destiny Books, 1999.

Maps of the Ancient Sea Kings: Evidence of Advanced Civilization in the Ice Age
Charles H. Hapgood, Souvenir Press Ltd, 2001.

The Meaning of the Dead Sea Scrolls: Their Significance for Understanding the Bible, Judaism, Jesus, and Christianity
James C. VanderKam and Peter W. Flint, HarperCollins, 2004.

Mosaics of Zeugma
Mehmet Onal, Milet Publishing Ltd, 2004.

Nazi Gold: The Sensational Story of the World's Greatest Robbery and the Greatest Criminal Cover-up
Douglas Botting and Ian Sayer, Mainstream Publishing, 2003.

The Orion Mystery: Unlocking the Secrets of the Pyramids
Robert Bauval and Adrian Gilbert, Crown Publishing Group, 1995.

The Phaistos Disc Alias the Minoan Calendar
OLE Hagen, AuthorHouse, 2001.

The Piri Reis Map of 1513
Gregory C. McIntosh, University of Georgia Press, 2000.

Queen of Sheba: Treasures from Ancient Yemen
St John Simpson (Editor), British Museum Press, 2002.

Quest for Discovery: The Remarkable Search for Noah's Ark
Richard Carl Bright, New Leaf Press, 2001.

Quest for the Dutchman's Gold: The 100-Year Mystery: The Facts, Myths and Legends of the Lost Dutchman Mine and the Superstition Mountain
Robert Sikorsky, Golden West Publishers, 1991.

The Riddle of the Rosetta Stone
James Cross Giblin, HarperTrophy, 1993.

Rosslyn: Guardian of Secrets of the Holy Grail
Tim Wallace-Murphy and Marilyn Hopkins, Element Books, 1999.

Schliemann of Troy: Treasure and Deceit
David A. Traill, St. Martin's Press, 1997.

Searching for El Dorado: A Journey into the South American Rainforest on the Tail of the World's Largest Gold Rush
Marc Herman, N.A. Talese, 2003.

The Search for El Dorado
John Hemming, Phoenix Press, 2001.

Searching for the Ark of the Covenant: Uncovering the Latest Discoveries
Randall Price, Harvest House Publishers, 2005.

Secret Chamber: The Quest for the Hall of Records
Robert Bauval, Arrow, 2000.

The Secret of Atlantis
Otto Heinrich Muck, Times Books, 1978.

The Secret Treasure of Oak Island: The Amazing True Story of a Centuries-Old Treasure Hunt
D'Arcy O'Connor, Lyons Press, 2004.

The Seven Wonders of the Ancient World
Peter Clayton, Martin Price, Routledge, 1990.

The Seven Wonders of the World: A History of the Modern Imagination
John Romer and Elizabeth Romer, Sterling Publishing Company, 2001.

Ship of Gold in the Deep Blue Sea
Gary Kinder, Atlantic Monthly Press, 1998.

Shipwrecks in the Americas
Robert F. Marx, Dover Publications, 1987.

Solomon: Falcon of Sheba: The Tombs of King Solomon & the Queen of Sheba Discovered
Ralph Ellis, Edfu Books, 2003.

The Templars and the Ark of the Covenant: The Discovery of the Treasure of Solomon
Graham Phillips, Bear & Company, 2004.

Ten Thousand Scorpions: The Search for the Queen of Sheba's Gold
Larry Frolick, McClelland & Stewart, 2003.

Timaeus and Critias
Plato, Penguin Books, 1971.

The Travels of Marco Polo (Wordsworth Classics of World Literature)
Marco Polo, Wordsworth Editions Ltd, 1997.

Troy and Homer: Towards a Solution of an Old Mystery
Joachim Latacz, Oxford University Press, 2004.

The Turin Shroud
Ian C. Wilson, Penguin Books, 1979.

Turin Shroud: In Whose Image? the Truth Behind the Centuries-Long Conspiracy of Silence
Lynn Picknett and Clive Prince, HarperCollins, 1994.

Veronica and Her Cloth: History, Symbolism, and Structure of a 'True' Image
Ewa Kuryluk, Blackwell Publishers, 1991.

PHOTO CREDITS